THE ECONOMICS OF PROPERTY RIGHTS AND NUISANCE LAW

By

David W. Barnes
Professor of Law, University of Denver

Lynn A. Stout
Professor of Law, Georgetown University

Reprinted from Barnes and Stout's "Cases and Materials on LAW AND ECONOMICS" (West, 1992)

AMERICAN CASEBOOK SERIES ®

WEST PUBLISHING CO.
ST. PAUL, MINN., 1992

Reprinted from Barnes and Stout's "Cases and Materials on LAW AND ECONOMICS" (West, 1992).

American Casebook Series and the WP symbol are registered trademarks of West Publishing Co. Registered in the U.S. Patent and Trademark Office.

COPYRIGHT © 1992 By WEST PUBLISHING CO.
610 Opperman Drive
P.O. Box 64526
St. Paul, MN 55164–0526

Library of Congress Cataloging-in-Publication Data

Barnes, David W.
   The economics of property rights and nuisance law / by David W.
Barnes, Lynn A. Stout.
     p.   cm. — (American casebook series)
   Includes index.
   ISBN 0–314–01088–2
   1. Property—Economic aspects—United States—Cases.
2. Nuisances—Economic aspects—United States—Cases. I. Stout,
Lynn A., 1957–   . II. Title. III. Series.
KF560.B37 1992
346.7303'6—dc20
[347.30636]   92–20399
                                   CIP

ISBN 0–314–01088–2

(B. & S.) Econ. of Prop. Rights ACB

Preface

During the past three decades, scholars wielding the tools of economics have marched through the curricula of American law schools, applying economic analysis to one substantive area of law after another. Accustomed to formal theoretical models of institutions and human behavior, "law and economics" scholars often examine legal rules in the abstract rather than discussing their application to specific cases. By contrast, conventional law teaching begins with specific cases and abstracts from those cases the general principles governing decisions. The series of books of which this one is a part combines the theory of economics and the pedagogy of law by exploring economic analysis of law primarily through reported judicial opinions and agency decisions. Excerpts from classic writings have been included to give a flavor for the type of discourse in which law and economics scholars engage.

Economic analysis is becoming a routine part of the consideration of policies underlying various substantive areas of law. This series provides cases and materials to supplement law school courses in which economic analysis is particularly relevant. Three books, *The Economics of Property Rights and Nuisance Law*, *The Economic Analysis of Tort Law*, and *The Economics of Contract Law*, focus on the economic analysis of common law courses typically taught in the first year of law school. *Economic Foundations of Regulation and Antitrust Law* presents an introduction to microeconomic theory in the context of government regulation of business, including cases and materials raising issues of occupational safety and health, environmental regulation, postal regulation, cable television, and consumer protection, along with tax and antitrust cases. *The Economics of Constitutional Law and Public Choice* examines constitutional questions of equal protection, due process, separation of powers, voting rights, the police power, and judicial review, among others. All of the books in the series are designed for readers with no prior economic training.

The books exploring the economic implications of common law doctrines all include an introduction to the basic economic assumptions of rationality and scarcity and the concepts of utility maximization, wealth maximization, and allocative efficiency. They deal with the three areas of law that virtually all law students study in their first year of law school: property, torts (personal injury), and contracts. The books encourage the reader to examine the implications and appreciate the relevance of economic analysis by using the familiar case method.

iii

The Economics of Property Rights and Nuisance Law explores alternative ways of defining property and protecting property rights, reasons for adopting private rather than communal property, and mechanisms for resolving conflicting uses of property. The Coase Theorem and Calabresi and Melamed's characterizations of alternative types of property and how property rights should be assigned and protected are central themes that run throughout the book. The legal treatment of externalities arising from conflicting land use is treated in detail. In addition, the economic theory of the Tragedy of the Commons and its game theory counterpart, the Prisoner's Dilemma, are used to analyze the choice between common and private ownership. Traditional property law issues discussed in this book include the meaning of property rights, adverse possession, easements, restrictive covenants, and nuisance law.

The case orientation of these books should appeal to those eager to escape the artificial assumptions often associated with economics, as well as those eager to explore the ethical and distributional dimensions of law. Analyzing reported decisions requires economics to come to grips with reality and emphasizes the implausibility of assumptions frequently made to facilitate economic analysis. Real rather than hypothetical factual contexts also highlight the distributional and ethical implications of economic analyses of law. Rather than gloss over such issues, the books in the series regularly raise the normative implications of particular legal rules. *The Economics of Property Rights and Nuisance Law*, for instance, considers the efficiency and distributional implications of alternative forms of property rights and of different methods of protecting property rights. *The Economic Analysis of Tort Law* draws the reader's attention to the distributional implications of alternative measures of damages. *The Economics of Contract Law* considers contract law's bias in favor of the status quo from which bargaining takes place and the implications of unequal bargaining power. *Economic Foundations of Regulation and Antitrust Law* contracts an antitrust policy that focuses on allocative efficiency to a policy that focuses on the welfare of consumers as a class. The analysis of constitutional law in *The Economics of Constitutional Law and Public Choice* focuses on the distribution of power among society's members and the distributional implications of alternative mechanisms for institutionalizing state coercion. These books are vehicles for appreciating and critically examining, rather than merely promoting, the economic analysis of law.

Most footnotes and citations contained in reported opinions and other quoted materials have been omitted without any indication. In the rare occasions where such footnotes have been included, they are reproduced with their original numbering. All other omissions from excerpted texts are indicated by asterisks.

Acknowledgments

The authors would like to thank the publishers and authors of the following works for allowing them to include excerpts in this text or in *Cases and Materials on LAW AND ECONOMICS*, from which this text is derived:

J. Buchanan & G. Tullock, The Calculus of Consent: Logical Foundations of Constitutional Democracy 63–72, 77–78, 81 (1962). Copyright © 1962 by the University of Michigan Press. Reprinted with permission.

Calabresi and Melamed, Property Rules, Liability Rules, and Inalienability: One View of the Cathedral. 85 Harv.L.Rev. 1089, 1092–93, 1105, 1111–15 (1972). Copyright © 1972 by the Harvard Law Review Association. Reprinted with permission.

Coase, The Problem of Social Cost, 3 J. Law & Econ. 1–2, 13 (1960). Copyright © 1960 by the University of Chicago, University of Chicago Press. Reprinted with permission.

Easterbrook, Ways of Criticizing the Court, 95 Harv.L.Rev. 802, 811–16, 818–19, 831 (1982). Copyright © 1982 by the Harvard Law Review Association. Reprinted with permission.

Hardin, The Tragedy of the Commons, 162 Science 1243, 1244–45 (December 13, 1968). Copyright © 1968 by the American Association for the Advancement of Science. Reprinted with permission.

Posner, Gratuitous Promises in Economics and Law, 6 J. Legal Studies 411–13 (1977). Copyright © 1977 by the University of Chicago, University of Chicago Press. Reprinted with permission.

Priest, The Common Law Process and the Selection of Efficient Rules, 6 J. Legal Studies 65–73, 81–82 (1977). Copyright © 1977 by the University of Chicago, University of Chicago Press. Reprinted with permission.

J. Rawls, A Theory of Justice 3–4, 11, 12, 13, 14–15, 22, 60–62, 136–37, 140–41, 151–53 (1971). Copyright © 1971 by the President and Fellows of Harvard College, Harvard University Press. Reprinted with permission.

Shavell, Strict Liability Versus Negligence, 9 J. Legal Studies 1–3, 22–23 (1980). Copyright © 1980 by the University of Chicago, University of Chicago Press. Reprinted with permission.

Williamson, Economics As An Antitrust Defense Revisited, 125 U.Pa.L.Rev. 699, 704, 706–708 (1977). Copyright © 1977 by The University of Pennsylvania. Reprinted with permission.

*

Summary of Contents

*

Table of Contents

Table of Cases

The principal cases are in bold type. Cases cited or discussed in the text are roman type. References are to pages. Cases cited in principal cases and within other quoted materials are not included.

*

*

THE ECONOMICS OF PROPERTY RIGHTS AND NUISANCE LAW

*

Chapter 1

INTRODUCTION

The law is designed to resolve the conflicting claims that arise when people interact in society. Benefits from the use and ownership of property, from promises based on contracts, and from engaging in activities that present risks to others are accompanied by corresponding burdens: the burden of being excluded from another's property, the obligation to perform one's own promises, and the risk of injury caused by another's activity. Legal rules allocate the benefits and burdens of social interaction, following complex, everchanging, and sometimes unfathomable doctrines.

Economics also is concerned with how to resolve competing claims. While there are economists evaluating law from all political perspectives, many take the traditional or neo-classical perspective that allocates the benefits and burdens of a legal rule according to a single principle, *economic efficiency*. Given the appeal of a single principle on which to base judgments regarding the propriety of legal rules and the fact that both law and economics are concerned fundamentally with the same questions, it is not surprising that lawyers and legal scholars have looked to economics for guidance in evaluating the wisdom and likely effects of legal rules.

This casebook introduces the basic concepts of economics and applies them to legal problems. Economic analysis can shed light on the consequences of the law's murky operations by focusing on the incentives created by the law. Applying economic principles to legal problems brings a better understanding of the implications of legal rules.

A. EFFICIENCY AND UTILITY MAXIMIZATION

Economics studies rational choice in a world of scarcity. The fundamental goal of economic analysis is getting the most from the

1

scarce resources available to satisfy society's needs and wants by allocating them efficiently among competing uses. The meaning of these terms—rational choice, scarcity, and efficiency—are explored in the following cases, which illustrate a variety of ways in which personal and real property is allocated.

CIDIS v. WHITE

District Court, Nassau County, Fourth District, 1972.
71 Misc.2d 481, 336 N.Y.S.2d 362.

GITELMAN, JUDGE.

In this action, plaintiff, a duly licensed optometrist, was requested by defendant, Carol Ann White, an infant, 19 years of age, to furnish her with contact lenses. She advised plaintiff that she urgently desired them as soon as possible. She agreed to pay $225.00 for the lenses and gave the doctor her personal check for $100.00. Plaintiff, accordingly, after examining infant defendant's eyes immediately ordered the lenses from his laboratory and incurred an indebtedness of $110.00. The examination was held on Thursday evening, the lenses were ordered on Friday, and received by the doctor on Saturday. On Monday morning the infant called and disaffirmed her contract on advice and insistence of her father, and stopped payment on her check. The infant was 19 years of age, working, and although living at home with her parents, paid for her room and board.

The plaintiff established that the contact lenses could be used by no one but the infant and have no market value at all, thus resulting in an absolute loss to the plaintiff of $110.00.

The question presents itself as to whether or not the contact lenses were "necessaries." The term "necessaries" as used in the law relating to the liability of infants therefor is a relative term, somewhat flexible, except when applied to such things as are obviously requisite for the maintenance of existence, and also depends on the social position and situation in life of the infant.

An analogy may be drawn between the instant case and the situation that existed in the case of Vichnes v. Transcontinental & Western Air, Inc. and in Bach v. Long Island Jewish Hospital. In the *Vichnes* case an infant purchased a round trip ticket to California and after using it tried to disaffirm and recover the money he paid. The Appellate Term reversed the Municipal Court and dismissed his claim. In the *Bach* case, an emancipated infant attempted to disaffirm her consent to a cosmetic operation performed on her. The Supreme Court, Nassau County, refused to permit her to do so. In both of these cases, the infant had received full benefit and could not place the defendant in status quo. So also in this case, since the contact lenses are of no value to anyone except the infant defendant, the plaintiff has suffered a loss and cannot be put back in status quo except by payment of a reasonable sum.

The Court has in mind the case of International Text Book Co. v. Connelly, which holds that an infant is not liable for a sum in excess of the fair value of the necessaries furnished even though he has contracted to pay more.

Accordingly, and for the purpose of doing substantial justice between the parties, judgment is granted in favor of the plaintiff and against the defendant, Carol Ann White, in the sum of $150.00. Since the defendant, Carol Ann White, is emancipated, no judgment may be granted against her father, the defendant, Richard A. White, and accordingly the complaint is dismissed as to him. During the trial the father urged that his daughter should not be penalized for obeying her father. The Court suggests that there is nothing to prevent the father from paying the judgment for his daughter, if he is so minded.

Notes and Questions

1. The study of economics begins with assumptions about what motivates people to act. In *Cidis,* both White and Cidis apparently entered the contract voluntarily and deliberately—neither was forced to deal with the other. Given such facts, it seems likely that each entered the contract out of self-interest. Each expected to be happier, better-off, and more satisfied after the exchange.

Economists usually do not bother with why people desire certain things or whether they should desire those things at all. Recognizing and accepting that people find happiness in different ways, economists are more interested in *how* individuals pursue happiness, satisfaction, and fulfillment—what economists refer to as *utility.*

Question: Is it reasonable to suppose that both Cidis and White thought they were improving their own levels of utility when they struck their bargain, even though it is quite unlikely they actually thought of it in those terms?

2. Economists assume that people generally prefer more utility to less utility. Rational individuals therefore attempt to *maximize* their utility and extract the highest possible level of happiness from the limited resources available to them. Rational maximization requires more of people than simply striking bargains that leave them better off. To maximize her utility, Carol Ann White must use her presumably limited monetary resources to buy those items that bring her the *most* utility. It would be irrational for her to spend $225 on contact lenses if another use of the money—say, to purchase a stereo—would bring her even more happiness.

While White may have thought that she would gain the most utility by using her $225 to buy contact lenses, her father obviously had different ideas. Perhaps he thought his daughter's interests would be better served by using the money for school books or college tuition. In making such a decision, White's father implicitly recognized that the world is a place of *scarcity.* Valuable resources—including food, energy, land, time, and labor, not to mention Carol Ann's bankroll—are finite in amount. Allocating resources to one purpose often sacrifices the opportunity to use those resources for something else. Using clean air as a dumping ground for airborne pollutants interferes with using the air for healthy breathing. A government on a balanced budget must choose between spending money on nuclear weapons or social programs.

Economists refer to the opportunities foregone by choosing to use limited resources for another purpose as the *opportunity cost* of using the resources. By spending her $225 on contact lenses, White incurred the opportunity cost of not being able to spend that money on school books or college tuition. From an opportunity cost perspective, she gave up school books and tuition payments for the lenses. She rationally maximized her utility (was a *rational maximizer*) only if she valued the lenses more than the other opportunities she sacrificed.

Questions: What opportunity cost did Cidis incur when he spent his time providing contact lenses for White? Would Cidis be a rational maximizer if he could have used the same time to sell lenses to someone willing to pay more than White?

3. Scarcity and rationality provide the basis for understanding the concept of *efficiency*. Scarcity does not mean that every item desired is as hard to find as a flawless diamond. Scarcity in an economic sense means that the item's supply is sufficiently limited that not enough exists to satisfy all desires. The item must be allocated among competing uses. Rationality is more controversial, primarily because it is often misunderstood. Economists do not believe that everyone always acts rationally. People sometimes behave in an apparently self-destructive fashion. People sometimes make mistakes and are sometimes too tired or uninformed to choose wisely among alternatives. Economists do assume, however, that people *generally* attempt to make themselves as well-off as possible. Economists also recognize that sometimes people gain utility by making others better off as well.

When resources are scarce, rational maximizers want to use their resources to the best possible advantage—to "get the most" out of them. If people seek happiness or utility, allocating scarce resources efficiently means allocating them in a fashion that maximizes the happiness or utility people derive from them.

The exchange Cidis and White contemplated provides an example of an efficient reallocation that may increase the level of utility derived from scarce resources. No rational maximizer would give up one resource in exchange for another unless she valued the second resource more. If Cidis and White were rational maximizers, then at the time of the contract White valued the lenses more than the $225, and Cidis valued the money more than the lenses and the time needed to fit them. The exchange would not increase the total amount of resources available, but it would increase the total amount of utility those resources provided by making both Cidis and White feel better off. Thus, if Cidis and White were rational maximizers, it would have been efficient to allow them to reallocate their resources through exchange.

4. As the preceding note suggests, voluntary exchange can be an important means of efficiently redistributing resources so as to maximize utility. In most cases, the law respects and enforces voluntary contractual exchanges. In Cidis v. White, however, the court refused to require White

to perform the terms of her contractual obligation because, under New York State law, she was still a minor. The contracts of minors are generally regarded as voidable or unenforceable against the minor, although an adult who contracts with a minor will be bound. Even if the contract is for necessaries, a minor is liable only if she has actually used the necessaries or is for some other reason unable to return them so as to restore the merchant to the status quo. If Cidis had sought to enforce his contract with White before the lenses had been ordered from the laboratory, the contract would have been unenforceable.

Questions: Does the legal rule that minors lack capacity to enter binding contracts imply that utility maximization is unimportant, at least for minors? Might there be another explanation for the rule?

5. Denying minors the capacity to enter into binding contracts yet holding adult sellers to their promises might discourage adults from providing goods and services to minors. An exception to the incapacity rule is made for the provision of "necessaries," "such things as are obviously requisite for the maintenance of existence."

Question: Is this exception based simply on a desire to provide essential services to minors or on a conclusion that minors are more likely to be rational when it comes to necessities? Keep in mind the limitation on enforcement of a minor's contract that requires return of the "necessaries" or limits the amount the minor must pay to the "fair value" of the goods received.

6. When setting the fair value the minor must pay, the court is substituting its own judgment regarding an item's value for the voluntary bargaining of the parties.

Question: Under what circumstances could a court determination of the exchange price lead to an inefficient allocation of resources?

7. It is difficult for a decisionmaker (other than the parties to an exchange) to estimate how much utility other persons gain or lose as a result of an exchange. Of course, the decisionmaker can always ask the parties involved. But there may be reason to doubt the accuracy of a party's response when he is not required to "put his money where his mouth is." Consider Carol Ann White's incentives had the Court, after ruling that she was not bound by the contract, asked her what the "fair value" of the lenses was.

Because of the difficulty of estimating how much utility someone else derives from a particular good or service, economists prefer whenever possible to rely on the individual's behavior as the best measure of the value she attaches to that good or service. If individuals are rational maximizers, their behavior in choosing how to allocate their resources will be a reliable reflection of their values. If Carol Ann chooses to buy contact lenses rather than school books, that indicates Carol Ann gets more utility from the lenses. The economist's assumption that individuals' actual choices reflect their preferences and values is described as the *theory of revealed preferences.*

B. EFFICIENCY AND WEALTH MAXIMIZATION

Allocative efficiency means using scarce resources to the greatest possible advantage, "getting the most" out of them. Whether a particular use is efficient will depend, by definition, on what exactly one wants to gain or accomplish. One might wish to allocate resources so as to maximize the utility people derive from them in order to achieve the greatest overall level of happiness. While a laudable goal in theory, in practice utility maximization can be difficult to implement. No direct means of measuring utility exists. If Carol Ann White chooses to purchase contact lenses, presumably she derives utility from the lenses. Unfortunately, it is impossible to know how *much* utility she derives. There is no ready way to measure how many "utils" Carol Ann gleans from contact lenses as opposed to textbooks, much less compare the value of one person's utils to another person's.

One can measure, however, the amount of money Carol Ann is willing to pay for her lenses. If Carol Ann decides to spend $225 on contact lenses but would only pay $100 for school books, one can determine not only that Carol Ann values the lenses more than the books, but also that she values the lenses at least $125 more. Individuals' willingness to pay money for particular goods can serve as a rough indicator of the value they attach to those goods. The more money a person is willing to pay for something, the more utility she expects to derive from it and the more she values it. Perhaps it is sensible to pursue a policy of maximizing wealth (the dollar value of scarce resources as measured by individuals' willingness and ability to pay for them) instead of maximizing utility.

ROSS v. WILSON

Court of Appeals of New York, 1955.
308 N.Y. 605, 127 N.E.2d 697.

VAN VOORHIS, JUDGE.

The controversy in this proceeding concerns the sale of the schoolhouse which served common school district No. 1 of the Towns of Ellicott and Gerry, in Chautauqua County, before it was superseded by a central school district. This district had been known as the Ross Mills District. In February, 1953, the board of education of the recently formed central school district called a special meeting of the qualified voters of the former common school district to vote upon whether to close the school and sell the school property. Such procedure is required by subdivision 6 of section 1804 of the Education Law, which also provides that if the common school district schoolhouse is sold, the net proceeds be apportioned among the taxpayers of the common school district.

At the special meeting of the common school district called by the board of education in 1953, four propositions were submitted: (1)

Should the school of the former common school district be closed? (2) Should the school property be sold to Ross Mills Church of God for $2,000? (3) Should the property be sold to Ross Grange No. 305 for $3,000? (4) Should the property be sold by public auction to the highest bidder? The notice stated that proposition number 1 would be voted upon, "and as many of the succeeding propositions as is necessary to dispose of the property". At the meeting, the proposal to close the school was carried. A motion was then made but declared out of order that the meeting should next ballot upon whether to sell the school property at public auction to the highest bidder. Then proposition number 2 was presented to the meeting to sell the school property to Ross Mills Church of God for $2,000. It was carried by a vote of 32 to 24. That ended the meeting.

* * * [S]ubdivision 6 of section 1804 of the Education Law, pursuant to which this schoolhouse was sold, does not expressly state that it must be sold to the highest bidder upon the organization of a central school district. * * *

* * *

* * * But if the Legislature does not require a schoolhouse to be sold at public auction, it by no means follows from that circumstance that the Legislature intended to authorize the public officials charged with the administration of school property, or even the majority of qualified electors voting at a school district meeting, to sell the property for a smaller amount than has been offered with due formality by a proper purchaser for a lawful use. * * * Whichever procedure is prescribed by the Legislature for selling this publicly owned property, it was the duty of the board of trustees and of the district meeting to obtain the best price obtainable in their judgment for any lawful use of the premises. In this respect, their powers and duties are similar to those of trustees. * * *

* * *

The amount of money involved is small, but the principle is important; the offer which was rejected was to pay 50% more for this schoolhouse than the one which was accepted. Bogert, writing on Trusts and Trustees, says (§ 745): "Whether the trustee should endeavor to sell by negotiation with possible buyers, or should put the property up at auction, depends upon the circumstances of the individual case. He should use the method which will, considering the place of sale and the type of property for sale, be apt to bring the best price." In the present situation, the Legislature has determined that it was not necessary to sell this property at auction, although that procedure would have been permissible, but the latitude allowed in the method of sale was designed to enable these public fiduciaries to adopt the method which in their judgment would bring the best price, and it was their duty to sell at the best price which it brought, not deliberately to select and to favor a buyer at a lower price than was otherwise obtainable. * * *

* * *

* * * The direct result of what occurred is, in effect, to approve a contribution of $1,000 by the school district to the church.   * * *

This contribution by a common school district to a particular church is not made in aid of any educational activity conducted by the church, but operates as an outright gift of public funds to a church for its general church purposes. Even if the facts of the case did not present the special situation of the use of public money for the support of a religious establishment, neither a common school district meeting, nor the district trustees, are empowered to expend the resources of the school district for other than educational objects. * * *

* * *

For the reasons mentioned, we think that there was a total lack of power in the school district to accept an offer of $2,000 from the Church of God of Ross Mills and at the same time to reject an equally bona fide offer of $3,000 from the grange. * * * The order appealed from should be reversed and the determinations of the Commissioner of Education and of the board of education approving the sale to the Church of God of Ross Mills should be annulled, with costs to appellants in this court and in the Appellate Division.

* * *

Notes and Questions

1. The resource to be allocated in *Ross* was a schoolhouse no longer required for educational purposes. Buildings are scarce and the schoolhouse potentially could serve various other needs. Wealth maximizing would require the schoolhouse to be allocated to the group or individual who valued it most highly, as measured by willingness to pay money for it.

Between a willing buyer and seller, it is easily determined who values the schoolhouse more. If the buyer is willing and able to pay enough to induce the seller to part with the building, the buyer must attach a higher dollar value to the building than the seller does. Thus, the school district's sale of the schoolhouse to the Ross Mills Church of God for $2,000 would increase the monetary value of the schoolhouse. In *Ross,* the bargain between the School District and the Church of God did not mean the schoolhouse would go it its *most* valuable use, only that it would go to a *more* valuable use. Another potential buyer may be willing and able to pay even more; in this case, the Grange had offered $3,000. Negotiations among all parties interested in purchasing the schoolhouse—including the Ross Mills Church of God, the Grange, and any other bidders—would reveal who was willing to pay the highest price, and so valued the schoolhouse the most.

Questions: How did the school district's decision to ignore the Grange's offer and sell the schoolhouse to the Church of God for $2,000 interfere with maximizing wealth—i.e., the value of resources as measured by people's willingness to pay for them? Did the school district's decision to sell to the Church of God for $2,000 really amount to a "contribution" to the Church of $1,000? Would the Church of God have been better or worse off if the Grange had only bid $1,999?

2.   The notes following *Cidis* examined how voluntary exchange can efficiently redistribute resources in a fashion that increases overall utility. As *Ross* illustrates, voluntary exchange can also increase wealth. Indeed, voluntary negotiations among all interested parties can *maximize* wealth by ensuring that a particular resource is allocated to the highest bidder who, by definition, values the resource the most as measured by willingness to pay.

To appreciate wealth maximization, it may be useful to envision society's wealth as a pie. Other things being equal, a larger pie is preferable to a smaller one because there is more wealth to divide among society's members. Among economists, the Gross Domestic Product (GDP) is a familiar measure of the total value (wealth) of the goods and services produced in the United States during a given time period. It measures the quantity of goods and services produced and the values actually placed upon them, in terms of the prices paid for them. If in a given year the total goods and services produced yields a higher value, then the GDP increases, and society has more wealth.

The GDP may be too narrow a measure of social well-being because many scarce resources allocated by society are not included in the "goods and services" category. Goods such as clean air, privacy, and leisure time are rarely traded in the marketplace but are desirable and scarce commodities that people would be willing to bargain for and exchange if markets existed. A more comprehensive measure of the size of the social "pie" would reflect all the items people value, not just goods and services traded on organized markets. Thus, the goal of wealth maximization should perhaps be the greatest possible "gross domestic valuation" or "GDV." GDV is maximized and society is best off when every resource—tangible and intangible, market and non-market—goes to its highest-valued use.

Ross typifies most cases in which the court exhibits no conscious concern for wealth maximization as a social goal and no explicit recognition of the social implications of arrangements that interfere with the parties' ability to bargain freely over the purchase and sale of scarce resources. Rather, the court seems concerned only with the taxpayers' rights and the apparent unfairness of depriving them of the ability to obtain the best price for their property.

> *Questions:* Suppose that in open bidding the prosperous farmers who belong to the Ross Grange were willing to offer $3,000 for the schoolhouse, while the impoverished members of the Ross Mills Church were only willing to pay $2000. Would that necessarily mean that the Grange's members would derive more utility from the schoolhouse? Would the auction system maximize utility?

3.   If some allocations might be wealth maximizing but not utility maximizing (and vice versa), one should be careful in choosing what to maximize. This Chapter has already explored some of the difficulties of adopting utility maximization as a goal. In particular, it is impossible to gauge even one person's level of utility or satisfaction. Even if it were possible, one cannot compare the value of one person's utils to another

person's utils.   In addition to the problems of measuring and making interpersonal comparisons of utility, utility maximization also has undesirable distributional implications.   Some people may have a greater capacity to enjoy life and derive satisfaction from scarce resources.   Following the principle of utility maximization, resources would be allocated to those happy-go-lucky individuals who have a greater capacity for enjoyment while dour and impossible-to-satisfy law or economics professors would go without any resources.

Wealth maximization avoids some of the measurement problems associated with utility maximization.   Although one may not trust what people always *say* about how highly they value a particular good or service, one can usually trust their behavior when they express their willingness (and ability) to pay through the actual purchase or sale of resources.   Moreover, while the utils of two people are not comparable, one person's dollar is as valuable as another's.   Money thus provides a common measuring rod for comparing the relative values that different persons attach to particular resources.

Because wealth is much easier to quantify than utility, economists customarily use individuals' relative willingness and ability to pay money to judge the propriety of a particular reallocation of resources.   But defining the value of a resource according to peoples' willingness and ability to pay for it also has distributional implications.   Wealth maximizing inevitably requires that a greater share of resources go to wealthier people.   Even if the poor congregation of the Ross Mills Church of God coveted the schoolhouse while the prosperous farmers of the Grange only mildly preferred it, the Grange's greater wealth might enable the farmers to outbid the Church.

Questions: If the New York Court of Appeals had upheld the school district's decision to sell the schoolhouse to the Ross Mills Church of God for $2,000, can one be certain that that decision would interfere with wealth maximization, i.e., prevent the schoolhouse from going to its most valuable use?   Might a subsequent *reallocation* correct the inefficiency resulting from the school district's decision?

4.   In an earlier appeal before the New York Commissioner of Education, the Commissioner had upheld the district's discretion to sell to a lower bidder on the ground that "[t]he type and character of the purchaser * * * is often a matter of vital import to the rural communities of this State.   * * * If the sale were mandated to be to the highest bidder, it may well be that a 'saloon', filling station or other enterprise undesirable to a specific community might be forced upon it."   127 N.E.2d at 699.

Suppose that the Grange would derive more utility from the schoolhouse than the Church, and the Grange was willing and able to pay more than the Church.   Does this mean that the Grange's use of the schoolhouse is the most valuable use?   Others in the community might be affected by the sale of the schoolhouse to the Grange, as they might be affected by the sale to a saloon.   Those adversely (or positively) affected by the sale to a particular party might even be willing and able to express their desires by paying to ensure that the schoolhouse went to a particular party.

Question: If the preferences of parties adversely (or positively) affected by a sale are not taken into account, does a decision to sell the schoolhouse to the highest bidder necessarily maximize utility? Wealth?

C. COMPARING UTILITY AND WEALTH MAX-IMIZATION: THE PARETO CRITERIA AND THE ROLE OF COMPENSATION

Both utility and wealth maximization share a common feature—judgments as to the desirability of allocations depend on the initial distribution of certain characteristics among society's members. For utility maximization, the characteristic is the capacity to derive happiness, pleasure, or satisfaction; in the case of wealth maximization, the characteristic is wealth. Many find the implications of relying for policy purposes on initial distributions of capacity to derive pleasure or of wealth troubling. A classification scheme designed by Vilfredo Pareto in the early 1900's provides one solution to this problem and also to the analytical difficulties presented by the impossibility of interpersonal utility comparisons. A neutral, nonjudgmental method for identifying desirable allocations and changes in the allocation of goods, Pareto's system still enjoys wide-spread use because of its appealing and generally accepted criteria for judgment.

The first application of the Pareto criteria is to evaluate the desirability of *changes* in the distribution of goods. Pareto's system allows that evaluation without regard to the desirability of the *initial* distribution among individuals of either their abilities to pay or enjoy and without the need for interpersonal utility comparisons. Imagine a society in which all resources have already been allocated to particular individuals. Now imagine a change in allocations that left at least one person better off and no one worse off. Surely that change is desirable from any perspective. Economists refer to such a change in the allocation of resources as a *Pareto superior* change.

The voluntary exchange of goods or services for money or other goods or services is a simple example of a Pareto superior reallocation of rights. The optometrist, Cidis, only agreed to sell the contact lenses to Carol Ann White because he valued the $225 more than the lenses and the labor required to fit them. White agreed to buy the lenses because she thought she would be better off with them than with the $225. At least one party is better off, probably both. If the parties are acting rationally and no one else is adversely affected by the sale, only a misanthrope would prefer the original allocation of resources to the reallocation.

Any reallocation of resources that leaves at least one person worse off is described as *Pareto inferior*. If Cidis is forced to give the lenses to White without charge, then she is better off but he is worse off. From a utility maximizing perspective, one cannot say that her gain in utility is greater than his loss in utility. Because one person is worse off, economists conclude that the change is Pareto inferior to the prior allocation.

Pareto superiority and inferiority are ways of evaluating changes in allocations; a reallocation is Pareto superior if at least one party is made better off and no one is made worse off, but Pareto inferior if at least one party is made worse off. A second common use of Pareto's system is to evaluate allocations themselves rather than changes in allocations. *Pareto optimal* describes a characteristic of an allocation rather than a reallocation.

An allocation of resources is Pareto optimal if there is no possible reallocation that could make at least one person better off without making someone worse off. Suppose that society has allocated its resources so that Cidis has the contact lenses (along with the skill to fit them) and White has $225. If Cidis is willing to fit and sell the lenses for $225 and White is willing and able to pay that price, this original allocation is *not* Pareto optimal because a later exchange (reallocation) could make someone person better off without making anyone worse off. Now suppose that White buys the lenses for $225. Now no reallocation could make anyone better off without making someone worse off. If the contact lenses are with the person who values them most, then no one will be willing and able to pay her enough to make her give them up. That is Pareto optimal; optimal since all resources are going to their highest valued use; "Pareto" optimal because no further Pareto superior reallocations are possible.

Given a limited amount of resources, it is possible for more than one Pareto optimal allocation to exist. Suppose Cidis owns the contact lenses and has the skills required to fit them, while White strongly desires the lenses but does not have $225. The allocation of the lenses to Cidis is Pareto optimal because White cannot be made better off (by giving her the lenses) without making Cidis worse off. Yet, if the lenses are initially allocated to White, that allocation may also be Pareto optimal, since White cannot give Cidis the lenses without making herself worse off and White may be unwilling to sell them to Cidis for any price he would be willing to pay.

Although Pareto's system of evaluating allocations and reallocations of resources is widely accepted, its practical value is limited. The Pareto criteria for evaluating changes in allocations are quite strict: if a million people benefit and one is harmed, the reallocation is still Pareto inferior. If many different allocations of resources pass the test of Pareto optimality, how can one determine which allocation is best? United States v. Causby examines one possible method of expanding the usefulness of Pareto's classifications: compensation for forced reallocations.

UNITED STATES v. CAUSBY

Supreme Court of the United States, 1946.
328 U.S. 256, 66 S.Ct. 1062, 90 L.Ed. 1206.

DOUGLAS, JUSTICE.

* * *

Respondents own 2.8 acres near an airport outside of Greensboro, North Carolina. It has on it a dwelling house, and also various outbuildings which were mainly used for raising chickens. The end of the airport's northwest-southeast runway is 2,220 feet from respondents' barn and 2,275 feet from their house. The path of glide to this runway passes directly over the property—which is 100 feet wide and 1,200 feet long. The 30 to 1 safe glide angle approved by the Civil Aeronautics Authority passes over this property at 83 feet, which is 67 feet above the house, 63 feet above the barn and 18 feet above the highest tree. * * *

* * * Since the United States began operations in May, 1942, its four-motored heavy bombers, other planes of the heavier type, and its fighter planes have frequently passed over respondents' land buildings in considerable numbers and rather close together. They come close enough at times to appear barely to miss the tops of the trees and at times so close to the tops of the trees as to blow the old leaves off. The noise is startling. And at night the glare from the planes brightly lights up the place. As a result of the noise, respondents had to give up their chicken business. As many as six to ten of their chickens were killed in one day by flying into the walls from fright. The total chickens lost in that manner was about 150. Production [of eggs] also fell off. The result was the destruction of the use of the property as a commercial chicken farm. Respondents are frequently deprived of their sleep and the family has become nervous and frightened. Although there have been no airplane accidents on respondents' property, there have been several accidents near the airport and close to respondents' place. These are the essential facts found by the Court of Claims. On the basis of these facts, it found that respondents' property had depreciated in value. It held that the United States had taken an easement over the property on June 1, 1942, and that the value of the property destroyed and the easement taken was $2,000.

* * *

* * * [T]he United States conceded on oral argument that if the flights over respondents' property rendered it uninhabitable, there would be a taking compensable under the Fifth Amendment. It is the owner's loss, not the taker's gain, which is the measure of the value of the property taken. Market value fairly determined is the normal measure of the recovery. And that value may reflect the use to which the land could readily be converted, as well as the existing use. If, by reason of the frequency and altitude of the flights, respondents could not use this land for any purpose, their loss would be complete. It would be as complete as if the United States had entered upon the surface of the land and taken exclusive possession of it.

We agree that in those circumstances there would be a taking. Though it would be only an easement of flight which was taken, that easement, if permanent and not merely temporary, normally would be the equivalent of a fee interest. It would be a definite exercise of complete dominion and control over the surface of the land. The fact that the planes never touched the surface would be as irrelevant as the absence in this day of the feudal livery of seisin on the transfer of real estate. * * * In the supposed case the line of flight is over the land. And the land is appropriated as directly and completely as if it were used for the runways themselves.

There is no material difference between the supposed case and the present one, except that here enjoyment and use of the land are not completely destroyed. But that does not seem to us to be controlling. The path of glide for airplanes might reduce a valuable factory site to grazing land, an orchard to a vegetable patch, a residential section to a wheat field. Some value would remain. But the use of the airspace immediately above the land would limit the utility of the land and cause a diminution in its value. * * *

* * * The airplane is part of the modern environment of life, and the inconveniences which it causes are normally not compensable under the Fifth Amendment. The airspace, apart from the immediate reaches above the land, is part of the public domain. We need not determine at this time what those precise limits are. Flights over private land are not a taking, unless they are so low and so frequent as to be a direct and immediate interference with the enjoyment and use of the land. We need not speculate on that phase of the present case. For the findings of the Court of Claims plainly establish that there was a diminution in value of the property and that the frequent, low-level flights were the direct and immediate cause. We agree with the Court of Claims that a servitude has been imposed upon the land.

Notes and Questions

1. The reallocation of rights in *Causby* seems wealth maximizing since the government probably would have been willing to pay more for the use of the Causbys' airspace than the Causbys would have been willing to pay to keep it. The reallocation may even have been utility maximizing, though an informed guess is harder to make, because there is no easy way to compare (or even talk about) the pleasure or satisfaction lost by the chicken farmers and gained by the government. For a reallocation to be Pareto superior, however, neither party can be left worse off as a result. Without sufficient compensation to return the harmed party to her earlier position, the Pareto criteria for superiority will not be met. Full compensation ensures that the reallocation of airspace rights from the Causbys to the military was Pareto superior.

If a reallocation is Pareto superior, it increases both social utility and wealth. Consider the position of one party (the government in *Causby*) who is entitled to take another's property only after fully compensating the other. In *Causby,* the compensation awarded was $2,000. If that figure was properly calculated, the Causbys would suffer neither decreased utility nor reduced wealth from the taking. If either loss occurred, compensation was not truly "full." At this point, a rational government would only take the Causbys' property if the benefits exceeded $2,000. Should the government proceed with the taking, it must value the airspace more (get more utility from the airspace) than the $2,000. The efficient result is that government has more wealth and utility and the Causbys have no less.

Questions: Is the government more or less likely to take private property if compensation is not required? Are such uncompensated reallocations (takings) utility maximizing? Wealth maximizing?

2. The government in the taking context does not consciously consider the utility and wealth maximizing consequences of a reallocation any more than do private parties to an exchange. It is extremely unlikely that either the optometrist or the contact lens purchaser in *Cidis* actually considered the social implications of their exchange of resources or that the school district in *Ross* considered whether the sale to the Church affected the aggregate level of society's wealth. The beauty of the compensation requirement is that utility and wealth are maximized by people concerned only with their own well-being.

3. While full compensation is sufficient to guarantee that utility and wealth are maximized, it is not always necessary. A reallocation without compensation may also maximize utility and wealth. If a decisionmaker (such as a court or legislature) knows for certain which resource use generates the most utility or is valued most highly then compensation is unnecessary. Thus, in *Causby,* the court could have simply allowed the government to invade the Causby's airspace without paying any compensation.

Without compensation, however, it is difficult to ascertain which allocations are utility and wealth maximizing. The reallocation in *Causby* was almost certainly wealth maximizing. The loss of the Causby's chicken farm was a necessary sacrifice if the runway was to be used for military operations. During World War II, military operations were extremely important and valuable in promoting national interests of the United States. As measured by willingness and ability to pay, the value of the airspace for defense purposes would seem to be much greater than its value to the Causbys for quietly raising chickens. To ensure wealth maximization, it seems unnecessary to put this reallocation to the compensation test.

Because of the difficulties inherent in systematically comparing the Causbys' loss in utility to the nation's gain, however, it is harder to conclude that the reallocation is utility maximizing without compensation. It is easily said that all Americans should be pleased by the liberation of Europe from the Nazis. But one cannot rigorously compare the government's gain from using that runway to the Causby's loss when the government destroyed their livelihood and the peace and quiet of their family farm. The difficulty in comparing utility gains and losses among different people makes the compensation test more necessary to ensure that a reallocation maximizes utility.

4. The analytical difficulties inherent in utility maximization have led many scholars in law and economics to focus on wealth maximization. Since it is easier to measure, some find wealth a useful surrogate for utility. For others, wealth maximization's appeal rests on its own merits. Because maximizing wealth does not always maximize utility, however, several schools of thought in economics have emerged.

Under one school, the Pareto criteria are appropriate for judging whether a reallocation is efficient. This view implies that full compensation must be paid whenever a reallocation of resources would otherwise leave someone worse off. Without compensation, there is no way to be certain that the benefits enjoyed by the winning party outweigh the harm suffered by the loser.

Since many changes in policy involve making some people better off and some worse off, economists Kaldor and Hicks studied alternatives to the compensation requirement. Under the *Kaldor–Hicks* position, compensation need not be paid for a reallocation to be efficient. A reallocation is efficient if there is sufficient gain to create the *potential* for full compensation. As long as the winner gains more than the loser loses, the loser does not actually have to be paid.

Like Pareto's approach, the Kaldor–Hicks approach requires compensation that is "full," that is, enough compensation that the loser would be no worse off after the reallocation. If the winner would be willing and able to pay such "full compensation," then the reallocation meets the Kaldor–Hicks test and the compensation need not actually be paid. From the Kaldor–Hicks perspective, it is not necessary, or even desirable, that the compensation be paid; compensating everyone who suffers as a result of state action is complicated and expensive, and interferes with the government's everyday operation.

In *Causby,* the Paretian perspective would require that full compensation actually be paid in order to be certain that the benefit to the government from using the airspace over the chicken farm outweighed the Causbys' losses. Under the Kaldor–Hicks position, since it was obvious that the value of the airspace to a wartime military was greater than its value to the Causbys in raising chickens, compensation was unnecessary for the taking to be efficient.

A policy designed to ensure that the loser is "no worse off" inevitably requires a measure of the appropriate level of compensation. To be "no worse off," the loser must receive enough compensation to obtain the same level of utility as before the reallocation.

Questions: If the government would be willing and able to pay "full compensation" in *Causby,* does the Kaldor–Hicks approach maximize both utility and wealth? If the potential compensation for a taking is calculated by the property's fair market value, can a policy maker be assured that the Kaldor-Hicks criterion maximizes both utility and wealth?

5. The preceding note focused on the Pareto and Kaldor–Hicks criteria for evaluating reallocations of resources. To test your understanding of the utility and wealth maximization characteristics of these alternative tests, consider the following policy analysis. Suppose that the decisionmaker could establish the maximum each party was willing and able to pay for the airspace and found that the Government was willing and able to pay more. Following the Kaldor–Hicks requirement, the decisionmaker would then award the airspace to the Government, figuring that, since the Government was willing and able to pay more, it could potentially compensate the Causbys.

Questions: Would the decisionmaker's approach guarantee that both utility and wealth were maximized? Does the reallocation from the Causbys to the Government meet the Pareto and Kaldor–Hicks criteria for superior reallocations?

6. In this book, an efficient allocation of resources is one that cannot be improved in either the Paretian or Kaldor–Hicks sense. If an allocation is efficient, a reallocation that benefits one person more than it harms another is impossible and compensation is unavailable. When describing a change in the law as efficient, the Kaldor–Hicks convention is usually followed, although Pareto's approach is not abandoned. Pareto's approach is appealing for reasons unrelated to wealth or utility maximization. While economics typically has little to say about what is fair or just, Pareto's criteria are appealing from a fairness perspective; justice seems to require compensation of people who, like the Causbys, suffer from a governmental policy.

D. EFFICIENCY AND EQUITY

Economists usually resist identifying particular individuals or classes of people as the proper recipients of rights to use or consume certain resources. To seem more scientific and to increase the acceptability of their conclusions among people with diverse social and political perspectives, they work hard to preserve the appearance of neutrality in their analysis. Economic analysis typically focuses on determining which allocation of scarce resources maximizes wealth. Economics is generally concerned with efficiency, not fairness.

Focusing on efficiency rather than fairness does not make economics a neutral and unbiased exercise. Directing resources to their most valuable uses and measuring value according to willingness and ability to pay biases allocations towards those with the greatest ability to pay. Among individuals with equally strong desires to own a certain house, the individual with the greater willingness and ability to express that desire by giving up money or other resources is judged the highest-valuing user; allocating the resource to his use is, by definition, allocatively efficient. Because efficiency analysis proceeds from a preexisting set of endowments of wealth, it does not question whether the initial distribution of "abilities to pay" is proper.

PITSENBERGER v. PITSENBERGER

Court of Appeals of Maryland, 1980.
287 Md. 20, 410 A.2d 1052.

MURPHY, CHIEF JUDGE.

This is the first case in which we consider the constitutionality of Maryland's new legislation on property disposition in divorce and annulment * * *

* * *

John and Mary Pitsenberger were married on June 30, 1962, in Alexandria, Virginia. Five children were born as a result of the marriage. In August of 1978, Mary left the family home in Rockville, Maryland, taking two of the parties' five minor children and $10,000 from the parties' joint savings account. About one month later, the other three children went to live with Mary in a small three bedroom townhouse in Derwood, Maryland. Mary rented the house on a month-to-month lease, but she was informed that the lease would not be renewed after May of 1979. While living with Mary, the children remained enrolled in the neighborhood schools near the family home. Mary drove them to school each day.

On January 2, 1979, Mary filed a bill of complaint for a divorce *a mensa et thoro* on the grounds of constructive desertion in the Circuit Court for Montgomery County. She sought pendente lite custody of the children, child support, alimony and, pursuant to § 3–6A–06(d), an exclusive use and possession order for the family home and family use personal property (furniture, appliances, household furnishings and a 1973 Dodge Dart). On February 9, 1979, John filed his answer and a cross-bill of complaint for divorce *a mensa et thoro* on the grounds of desertion.

On February 16, 1979, a hearing was held before a domestic relations master to determine pendente lite the issues of child custody and support, alimony, and the need of the parties and the children to remain in the family home. Mary testified that she was on welfare and lacked funds to rent another house or apartment. Despite John's yearly salary of approximately $47,000, she said she had received no child support since August, 1978. With respect to alternative living arrangements, Mary explained that her mother's residence, a small three bedroom house in Alexandria, Virginia, provided insufficient living room for her family. The only other alternative was to stay at the three bedroom house of her brother-in-law and his wife and two children. Even if they could reside there on an emergency basis, she would have to drive each day from Bowie, Maryland, to the children's schools. * * *

The master recommended that Mary be awarded pendente lite custody of the minor children and that John pay $1,000 per month child support, as well as pay the mortgage, taxes and insurance for the family home. The master also recommended that Mary be awarded pendente lite use of the family home, the family personal property located in the home and the Dodge Dart * * *. These recommendations were adopted by the circuit court on May 23, 1979, and its order specified that Mary was awarded the *exclusive* use of the family home.

* * *

John * * * argues that § 3–6A–06 permits the unlawful taking of private property without just compensation in violation of the Fifth and Fourteenth Amendments of the United States Constitution, Article 24 of the Maryland Declaration of Rights, and Article III, section 40 of the Maryland Constitution. John contends that the use and possession order signed by the court on May 23, 1979, effectively takes his property by awarding Mary the exclusive use of the family home and family use personal property. John asserts that he is entitled to compensation in the amount of the fair market value of his possessory interest in the family home and for relocation expenses.

To constitute a taking in the constitutional sense, so that the State must pay compensation, the state action must deprive the owner of all beneficial use of the property * * * [I]t is not enough for the property owner to show that the state action causes substantial loss or hardship. John, as guardian of his minor children, is charged with their support, care and welfare. Because his children have the use of the family home and family use personal property, John is in fact using his property to properly house his children. John therefore has not been deprived of all beneficial use of his property. In sum, the use and possession order does not amount to a "taking" of private property in violation of the federal or state constitutions.

We thus conclude that Mary was properly awarded pendente lite use and possession of the family and family use personal property.

Notes and Questions

1. The Maryland statute applied in *Pitsenberger* required a divorce court to divide a couple's property "fairly and equitably." In *Pitsenberger,* fairness and equity apparently required that Mary keep the family home and car, while John be ordered to leave the home. Three possible approaches to the equity and fairness issue are discussed below.

a. *Just Desserts.* The property should be assigned to the most deserving spouse. This approach requires a definition of "deserving." Perhaps the home and car should be awarded to the person who wants to remain married. If, hypothetically, John wanted to remain married but Mary insisted on a divorce after beginning an adulterous liaison, Mary should get nothing. Alternatively, perhaps the spouse who needs the property most deserves it. In that case, the lion's share should go to unemployed Mary while salaried John gets little or nothing.

b. *Equality of Treatment.* After selling the home and car, the decisionmaker divides the proceeds evenly between the parties. Under this rule, the Pitsenbergers should share the market value of these possessions.

(B. & S.) Econ. of Prop. Rights ACB–

c. *Ratified Consent.* The court should award the property to the individual in whose name the property is held and enforce any reallocation to which the parties consented. Thus, the court should enter an order that the property in John's and Mary's names belonged to John and Mary respectively, but should approve any swaps the two might agree to make.

Questions: Which view of fairness most closely approaches wealth maximization? Which views most closely reflect or offend our sense of fairness or equity?

2. An efficiency perspective on this distributional question might suggest that the property should be awarded to the person willing and able to pay more for it.

Questions: If the court awarded the home and car to the person who valued the property more, to whom would the property probably be awarded? Would this be a wealth maximizing allocation of resources?

3. People's willingness and ability to pay to influence the allocation of resources such as the Pitsenberger's house naturally depends on their wealth. The allocation of John's income between Mary and John is quite likely to influence the value they place on the house. Because the distribution of wealth among people influences the allocations that result from bargaining, changes in the distribution of wealth may change the allocation of resources. Alternative allocations of John's salary will affect who gets the house.

Compare two allocations of John's salary. In the first, Mary is awarded none of his salary and, in the second, Mary is awarded 70% of his salary. Imagine that after these distributions of John's salary are made, the house is allocated to the person willing and able to pay the most for it. Under the first allocation, it is quite probable that John will get the house. Under the second, it is more likely that Mary will get the house.

Question: Do the alternative allocations of John's salary affect the efficiency of the allocation of the house?

4. Returning to the principle of ratified consent, suppose that, after much discussion, the parties agreed that Mary would be allowed to rent the house, car and other property for $200 per month from her welfare check.

Questions: Would enforcing such a solution be wealth maximizing? Would it be utility maximizing? Does the fact that both parties consent to this arrangement make it seem fairer?

Chapter 2

PROPERTY RIGHTS AND
NUISANCE LAW

The institution of private property is one of the foundations of the common law. A property right is a right to the control of a valuable resource, tangible resources such as land or automobiles as well as intangibles such as labor or a patentable idea. Control includes the right to use or consume a resource or to transfer it to another. The economic analysis of property law examines why and when property rights are created, how to protect such rights, and to whom such rights should be assigned.

A. EXTERNALITIES AND INEFFICIENCY

The law governing real property use is an obvious place to begin the journey into efficiency analysis. The market for the right to *possess* land provides a convenient focus for economists' bargaining orientation. As applied to property, however, the efficiency goal is to allocate each parcel of land to its most valuable *use*. While the familiar market in land sales readily accommodates bargaining to determine which user should possess a particular parcel, no comparably well-developed market exists to facilitate bargaining over which of several conflicting uses of neighboring parcels should prevail. As the following materials reveal, solutions to incompatible uses involve the allocation of property rights as well as common law and regulatory approaches.

1. INTERNALIZING EXTERNALITIES THROUGH DAMAGE AWARDS

ORCHARD VIEW FARMS, INC. v. MARTIN MARIETTA ALUMINUM, INC.

United States District Court Oregon, 1980.
500 F.Supp. 984.

BURNS, CHIEF JUDGE:

This diversity case is before the court on remand from the Ninth Circuit Court of Appeals for a retrial on the issue of punitive damages.

On March 31, 1971, Orchard View Farms, Inc. (Orchard View) filed this trespass action, seeking compensatory and punitive damages for injuries to its orchards between March 31, 1965 and the filing date. These injuries were alleged to have been caused by fluoride emitted from the aluminum reduction plant operated by Martin Marietta Aluminum, Inc. (the company or Martin Marietta). In April and May, 1973, the case was tried to a jury, which awarded Orchard View $103,655 compensatory damages and $250,000 punitive damages.

* * *

In essence, any business is socially obliged to carry on an enterprise that is a net benefit, or at least not a net loss, to society. * * *

In a world where all costs of production were borne by the enterprise, determining whether a firm produced a net benefit, or at least not a net detriment, to society would be as simple as examining the company's balance sheet of income and expenses. In the real world the task is more complex, because enterprises can sometimes shift a portion of their costs of production onto others. In the case of an industrial plant emitting pollution, those harmed by the emissions are, in effect, involuntarily bearing some of the firm's production costs.

Our society has not demanded that such externalized costs of production be completely eliminated. Instead, we tolerate externalities such as pollution as long as the enterprise remains productive: that is, producing greater value than the total of its internalized and externalized costs of production. A business that does not achieve net productivity is harmful to society, detracting from the standard of living it is designed to enhance. Because firms can sometimes impose a portion of their production costs upon others, the mere fact that a company continues to operate at a profit is not in itself conclusive evidence that it produces a net benefit to society.

Our system of law attempts to ensure that businesses are, on balance, socially beneficial by requiring that each enterprise bear its total production costs, as accurately as those costs can be ascertained. A fundamental means to this end is the institution of tort liability, which requires that persons harmed by business or other activity be compensated by the perpetrator of the damage. * * *

* * *

A business enterprise has a societal obligation to determine whether its emissions will result in harm to others. Because the damage from pollution can be difficult to perceive due to its subtle or incremental nature, and because it can be difficult to trace to its cause, the obligation of the enterprise extends not only to observation of property in the surrounding region but also to initiation and completion of unbiased scientific studies designed to detect the potential adverse effects of the substances emitted.

I find that the company failed to fulfill this obligation before or during the 1965–71 claim period by taking less than full cognizance of the damage inflicted upon the orchards and by generally shirking its responsibility to undertake competent scientific inquiry into the adverse effects of its emissions.

Notes and Questions

1. The court characterized the pollution in *Orchard View Farms* as an "externalized cost" of Martin Marietta's aluminum-making activities. A cost is "external to" or "outside of" an economic actor's decisionmaking if he is not required to account for it when maximizing his well-being. If it does not have to pay for the damage to Orchard View Farms, Martin Marietta does not need to consider that damage when deciding how to maximize profits from its aluminum production. Industrial pollution is a classic example of an external cost.

Externalities are costs imposed or benefits conferred on others as a result of an individual's activities that he is not required to (in the case of costs) or able to (in the case of benefits) take into account in his decisionmaking.

Questions: What is an example of an external benefit one landowner might confer on another? How do externalities affect the extent to which people impose costs and confer benefits on others?

2. Using their current technologies, the plaintiff cannot grow trees and the defendant cannot produce aluminum solely within their own parcels' boundaries without affecting their neighbors. The air the farm uses to nourish its trees is the same air Martin Marietta uses to carry away its airborne fluoride particles. Neither party is interested in possessing the other's land, so the allocation of the land is not at issue. The issue involves uses of land and the allocation of a second resource, the stream of air. It is not possible for both parties to use that stream of air compatibly using their current technologies. While the farm may be able to grow its trees under a dome with filtered air or the plant may be able to wash all of the fluoride particles out of its emissions, neither possibility is presented in this case. The issue is who gets the right to use the stream of air.

Questions: The plaintiff was awarded damages to compensate it for the harm to its trees from the fluoride particles. Does that mean that the use of the stream of air was been allocated to the farm? Does it mean that the farm's use of the air was the more highly-valued use?

3. Consider how the court in *Orchard View Farms* viewed its role in the process of achieving allocative efficiency: "Our system of law attempts to ensure that businesses are, on balance, socially beneficial by requiring that each enterprise bear its total production costs."

Questions: Is the court's task finding which use is more valuable? Or does the court merely enable other parties to determine which use is more valuable? Note how this compares to the court's role in United States v. Causby in Chapter 1. Did either court decide which use is the most valuable or did it merely facilitate the determination? If the court did not decide how resources were allocated, who did?

4. Imagine a transaction between a buyer and seller of one ton of aluminum ingot. The seller is willing to sell aluminum for no less than $4 a ton and the buyer is willing and able to pay as much as $4.50 a ton. An exchange appears to be Pareto superior. The difference between the values the buyer and setter attach to the aluminum appears to ensure that the costs of producing a ton of aluminum (the bauxite ore, the electricity, the labor) are outweighed by the benefit the ton provides to the buyer.

From *Orchard View Farms,* however, one of the costs of producing aluminum is damage to the neighboring farm. If forced to pay damages resulting from his pollution, the manufacturer might be unable to sell that ton of ingot at a price high enough to ensure a profit. Once all the costs are considered, the buyer may be unwilling to pay the full cost of a ton of aluminum. Without internalizing costs, an inefficiently large amount of aluminum may be produced.

Question: What damages should be awarded to ensure that the allocatively efficient amount of resources are devoted to aluminum production?

5. The court's main concern in *Orchard View Farm* was that the defendant pay for his external costs. The external costs need not be eliminated; as much pollution as is efficient may continue. An allocatively efficient level of output of aluminum will occur even if the plaintiff is not compensated, as long as the defendant gives up an amount equal to the external costs imposed. The determination of the amount of plaintiff's injury is critical to calculating the optimal level of payment the firm must internalize, however, and it seems only fair that the payment should go to the person who suffers. Damages give plaintiffs an incentive to provide evidence on the magnitude of the external costs.

Question: If the damages were calculated, paid, and then dumped into the ocean (after taking out the attorneys' fee, of course!), would the defendant still take the amount of its liability for damages into account in deciding how much to produce?

6. In some cases, particularly class actions for environmental harms, damages are paid into a fund dedicated to a public use. To create proper incentives for the polluter, however, it must be assured that the polluter does not benefit from such a fund.

Questions: If, instead of dumping the damages into the ocean or paying them to the plaintiff, the damages were paid into a drug rehabilitation program or the school budget in the town where the factory was located, would the payment of damages still provide the proper incentives to the polluter?

2. INTERNALIZING EXTERNALITIES THROUGH REGULATION

UNITED STATES v. CITY OF NIAGARA FALLS

U.S. District Court, Western District of New York, 1989.
706 F.Supp. 1053.

CURTIN, DISTRICT JUDGE.

* * *

* * * Defendant City of Niagara Falls [City] owns and operates a municipal sewerage system consisting of the WWTP [Niagara Falls Wastewater Treatment Plant] and a related ancillary wastewater and stormwater collection system, which includes the FST [Falls Street Tunnel]. The FST is a large, rock-hewn tunnel under the streets of Niagara Falls, New York, that for many years collected sewage, industrial waste, stormwater and groundwater and sent the combined flow to the WWTP for treatment prior to discharge into the Niagara River.
* * *

During the early 1970s, it became evident that the WWTP was discharging an unacceptably high amount of toxic pollutants into the river. On January 9, 1974, pursuant to Section 402(a) of the Clean Water Act, the Regional Administrator of the Environmental Protection Agency [EPA] issued defendant NPDES Permit No. NY0026336, effective January 30, 1975, which established the terms and conditions under which the City may discharge pollutants. Pursuant to that permit, a new system was constructed at the WWTP to allow for chemical-physical treatment of sewage, followed by carbon adsorption. Completed in early 1978 at an approximate cost of $61 million (75% of which was derived from federal grants, and 12.5% from state grants), the carbon treatment system failed in July, 1978. [While that system was being repaired, the City discharged untreated water through the FST directly into the river. After repairs, the City failed to redivert the water back through the Wastewater Treatment Plant. Plaintiffs brought suit for a permanent injunction ordering the City to redivert the water.]

* * *

* * * [T]he discharge is a violation of that part of the Clean Water Act fundamental to furthering the Act's major underlying purpose of "establish[ing] a comprehensive long-range policy for the elimination of water pollution," as well as the stated objectives "to restore and maintain the chemical, physical, and biological integrity of the Nation's waters," and to "preserv[e] ... the environment and ... [protect] ... mankind and wildlife from harmful chemicals." The untreated FST discharge, therefore, continues not merely in derogation of "the integrity of the permit process" * * *, but is a violation which undermines the substantive policies, purposes, and objectives of the Clean Water Act, a violation for which this court has already determined plaintiffs are entitled to relief. The instant case is thus one in which injunctive relief, if warranted on balancing the equities, is proper as a means of furthering those policies, purposes and objectives.

* * *

* * * The essential balance that must be struck is whether the harm to the environment caused by the FST discharge is outweighed by the engineering difficulties which the City would face, and the economic burden which the users of the City's sewer system would bear, should all or part of that discharge be ordered to be re-diverted through the WWTP for treatment.

* * *

* * * I am convinced that injunctive relief is appropriate in this case * * *. Accordingly, I find that the most prudent exercise of discretion under all of the circumstances presented would be to grant plaintiff's request for a permanent injunction ordering immediate re-diversion of the maximum portion of the FST flow that can now be accomplished [to the WWTP].

* * *

Notes and Questions

1. The Clean Water Act addresses the external costs of water pollution by limiting the pollutants that can be added to navigable waters by any source, a regulation comparable to limiting the amount of fluoride Martin Marietta can emit from its aluminum plant. Rather than relying on a liability system to internalize costs and thereby reduce externalities to an allocatively efficient level, the Clean Water Act simply prohibits undesirable pollution. It attempts to control the total by estimating the limitations that must be imposed on each pollution source in order to reach its goal. This solution substitutes the government's judgment for the private parties' in calculating the optimal amount of pollution. Economists usually assume that individuals can determine better than government bureaucrats the value individuals place on resources.

Question: What are the risks of using government directives to control external costs like pollution?

2. The Clean Water Act established a federal system of control over water quality in navigable waters. Without federal regulation of water pollution, states and municipalities could allow or prohibit pollution as they chose. To attract industry and development from neighboring areas, jurisdictions could compete by providing more lenient pollution laws.

Questions: In the context of the Clean Water Act, how does this competition lead to the inefficient allocation of resources? What are the states' incentives without federal intervention and how might they lead to inefficient overpollution?

3. The regulatory approach of the Clean Water Act supplements the common law rights of owners of property on waterways. Sections 850 and 850A of the Restatement (Second) of Torts detail the waterfront property owners' rights. Section 850 states:

> A riparian proprietor is subject to liability for making an unreasonable use of the water or a watercourse or lake that causes harm to another riparian proprietor's reasonable use of water or his land.

Section 850A (h) makes clear that one factor relevant when determining the reasonableness of a use is "the protection of existing values of water uses, land, investments and enterprises." Comment (a) to § 850A concludes that "It is usually unreasonable * * * for a new user to destroy existing values created by a use that was reasonable in its inception."

> *Question:* Translated into its application to waterways, does this Restatement rule lead to an efficient use of the common waterway?

4. Private ownership can encourage the efficient use of a resource when a single owner enjoys all the benefits, and suffers all the costs, of a particular use of that resource. In this situation, no external costs or benefits escape unnoticed. The second major economic advantage of a private property system is that it permits exchange. Bargaining allows resources to be exchanged among users who assign different values and allows rights to be transferred to those who value them most highly. In 1776, Adam Smith lauded this process of exchange in The Wealth of Nations:

> Every individual endeavors to employ his capital so that its produce may be of greatest value. He generally neither intends to promote the public interest, nor knows how much he is promoting it. He intends only his own security, only his own gain. And he is in this led by an invisible hand to promote an end which was no part of his intention. By pursuing his own interest he frequently promotes that of society more effectively than when he really intends to promote it.

The next section explores in greater detail the role of private property and exchange in resolving the externality problems arising from conflicting uses of resources.

3. INTERNALIZING EXTERNALITIES THROUGH PRIVATIZATION

Orchard View Farms and *City of Niagara Falls* provide examples of two different ways the law can reduce the risk of inefficient resource allocation due to externalities. Liability rules such as those applied in *Orchard View Farms* encourage individuals and businesses to consider the impact of their activity on others by making them liable for any external costs they impose. The regulatory scheme in *City of Niagara Falls* employs a judge, bureaucrat or other decisionmaker to evaluate the costs and benefits of using the resource in a particular way and then directly allocate the resource to its most valuable use.

A third potential means of internalizing externalities is *privatization*. If a single person owns a particular resource, he enjoys the benefits of careful management and suffers the costs of abuse—he will use the resource efficiently because both costs and benefits are now "internalized" rather than borne by someone else. Consider how privatization might prevent the "Tragedy of the Commons."

HARDIN, THE TRAGEDY OF THE COMMONS *
162 Science 1243, 1244–45 (December 13, 1968).

The tragedy of the commons develops this way. Picture a pasture open to all. It is to be expected that each herdsman will try to keep as many cattle as possible on the commons. * * * At this point, the inherent logic of the commons remorselessly generate tragedy.

As a rational being, each herdsman seeks to maximize his gains. Explicitly or implicitly, more or less consciously, he asks, "What is the utility to *me* of adding one more animal to my herd?" This utility has one negative and one positive component.

1. The positive component is a function of the increment of one animal. Since the herdsman receives all the proceeds from the sale of the additional animal, the positive utility is nearly +1.

2. The negative component is a function of the additional overgrazing created by one animal. Since, however, the effects of overgrazing are shared by all the herdsmen, the negative utility for any particular decision-making herdsman is only a fraction of –1.

Adding together the component partial utilities, the rational herdsman concludes that the only sensible course for him is to add another animal to his herd. And another; and another.... But this is the conclusion reached by each and every rational herdsman sharing a commons. Therein is the tragedy. Each man is locked into a system that compels him to increase his herd without limit—in a world that is limited. Ruin is the destination toward which all men rush, each pursuing his own best interest in a society that believes in the freedom of the commons. Freedom in a commons brings ruin to all.

* * *

In an approximate way, the logic of the commons has been understood for a long time, perhaps since the discovery of agriculture or the invention of private property * * *.

Notes and Questions

1. The "Tragedy of the Commons" occurs when a decisionmaker's act—adding another animal to the commons—produces a net benefit to the decisionmaker, but imposes such substantial external costs on others that the overall resulting losses outweigh the benefits of the act. Nevertheless, rational herdsmen may continue to add cattle to an overgrazed commons. They know that acting responsibly (not adding cattle) would only allow more self-interested herdsmen to add more. The commons would still be

overgrazed, and the self-sacrificing herdsman would be worse off for behaving responsibly.

2. The following example of cattle grazing in a common field illustrates how overproduction of cattle (or overgrazing of grass) will result from herdsmen's failure to internalize their overgrazing costs. Table 2–1 reflects the benefits from increasing the size of the cattle herd allowed to graze on the common. There is no direct cost to those who allow their cattle to graze. The only cost is to the commons, which loses grass and suffers wear and tear. Column 1 indicates different numbers of grazing cattle. Column 2 indicates how much weight each cow gains as a result of a week of grazing. Column 2 shows that, for some reason, perhaps the cattle's greater contentment, adding a second cow increases the weekly weight gain per cow from 7 to 9 pounds. After the second cow, however, the gain per cow per week declines due to the common's small size and the cows getting in each other's way competing for the best grass. Note that even with eight or nine cattle, they all continue to gain weight. Each of eight or nine people have an incentive to bring a cow to graze. At ten cattle, however, the common is overcrowded, the cattle fight, the field produces less grass, and the cattle lose weight each week. No individual has any incentive to bring a cow to this crowded common so the herd size will level off at nine cows.

Table 2–1

Tragedy of the Commons-Illustrated

(1)	(2)	(3)	(4)
	Weight Gain per Cow per Week from	Total Weight Gain per	Additional Beef for Society Due to Increasing Herd Size by
Number of Cattle	Grazing	Week	One Cow
1	7	7	7
2	9	18	11
3	8	24	6
4	7	28	4
5	6	30	2
6	5	30	0
7	4	28	–2
8	3	24	–4
9	1	9	–15
10	–1	–10	–19

An individual deciding whether to put his animal on the common will look at Column 2. That column shows that until there are nine cattle on the common, any person who grazes his cow there will benefit because the cow will gain weight. From a societal viewpoint, however, Columns 3 and 4 rather than Column 2 present the relevant information. Rather than considering individual gains from cattle grazing, the societal perspective considers the number of cattle appropriate to yield the greatest weight of cattle for society as a whole. Column 3 presents the total increase in weight of cattle per week. Column 4 indicates the additional pounds of beef due to increasing the herd size by one cow. Increasing the size from one to two, for instance, increases the total weight gain by seven pounds while increasing the size from three to four increases the total weight gain by four pounds. The total weight gain is greatest at five or six cattle, though adding the sixth cow contributes nothing additional to the weight of beef available to society. Adding cattle beyond six actually diminishes social welfare so the optimum from a social perspective is five or six.

Unlike the individual optimum, which focuses only on column 2, the social optimum accounts for the effect of adding additional cattle on the weight gain by other cattle. The addition of another cow has external effects on the cattle already there. Without recognition of these effects and limitation of the number of cattle, society will tend naturally towards the tragedy of inefficient overuse of the commons. The legal question is how to structure resource use so that the outcome is efficient. One arrangement that may resolve this inefficiency is private property.

Questions: If a single individual owned the commons and was deciding how many cattle to graze, would the private property owner's optimum be the same as the social optimum? If a single individual owned the common and rented it to those who wished to graze cattle on the commons in exchange for a percentage of the weight gain, what number of grazing cattle would generate the greatest profit for the landowner?

3. A second arrangement would be centralizing decisionmaking in a single authority.

Question: If a commune with centralized decisionmaking were to decide how many cattle should graze to gain the most beef, would the communal optimum resemble the private property optimum or the societal optimum?

4. Under a third institutional arrangement, the central authority permits the first cattle raiser to put his cow on the common, but any person who subsequently added an animal would have to pay damages for the decreased beef production of the cattle already there.

Question: Would this damages solution result in the same number of cattle grazing as the private property optimum or the social optimum?

5. Hardin's description of the Tragedy of the Commons as "remorseless" implies that people inevitably will refuse to recognize the obvious and curb their selfish instincts.

Question: If the herdsmen know that too many cattle spoil the commons, why does Hardin assume that they will not voluntarily refrain from pasturing too many animals?

6. The institution of private property can be regarded as a legal response to the problem of external costs. As the previous questions suggest, private property is not the only possible response to the abuse of a common resource. Water and atmospheric pollution by firms like Martin Marietta is as much an inefficient "tragedy" as the overgrazing of a common pasture. Yet the court in *Orchard View Farms* never suggests

that the solution is for Martin Marietta to pollute only the air immediately above its own property; in other words, create a right to "private" air.

The reason should be obvious. It is highly impracticable (if not impossible) to segregate the atmosphere into private "plots" of air at any reasonable expense. When deciding whether to create private rights to a common resource, one must consider whether it is efficient to do so. Creating private property rights—whether to land, water, air, or animals— will only be efficient when the benefits of doing so exceed the costs.

The principal benefit of private rights is the internalization of excessive external costs. Thus, creating a private right will only be beneficial when it cures some inefficiency. For example, dividing a common pasture into private plots might allow a society of herdsmen to increase beef production by 1,000 pounds, because private grazing eliminates overgrazing. If beef sells at $1 a pound, the potential benefit is $1,000.

To ignore the costs of creating property rights, however, would not be sensible. These might include the cost of identifying and/or segregating one owner's property from another's as well as the cost of enforcing the right. Herdsmen deciding to subdivide a common grazing area might have to consider the cost of building fences to identify their land and keep cattle from straying, and of hiring a marshall to settle disputes. If these costs exceed $1,000, common ownership, with all of its externalities, might be more efficient than private ownership.

Harold Demsetz illustrated this point with the history of private property rights among Native Americans. See, Demsetz, *Toward a Theory of Property Rights*, 57 Am. Econ. Rev. 347 (No. 2, 1967). With the arrival of the French and a commercial fur trade in Labrador, animal pelts became far more valuable. In response to overhunting of furbearing animals such as marten and beaver, the tribes of Labrador quickly developed a system of private rights to land that allowed one individual or family to exclude others from hunting the area.

In contrast, the tribes of the Plains did not develop private rights to land. While overhunting plains buffalo was a problem, to create and enforce a private right to hunt buffalo was costly; buffalo are migratory and ornery beasts, and it was far too expensive to fence them in. In contrast, hunting rights in Labrador could be established by simply blazing trees. Thus, the development of property rights depends as much on its costs as its benefits.

7. The court in *Orchard View Farms* allowed punitive damages to encourage plaintiffs' suits, which force defendants to internalize the costs of pollution. Fearing that the promise of compensation alone was insufficient, the court observed, at 500 F.Supp. 989:

> In the context of pollution, however, the tort system does not always operate smoothly to impose liability for compensatory damages. Among the difficulties encountered are * * * that the harm may be inflicted in small amounts upon a large number of people, none of whom individually suffer sufficient damage to warrant the time and expense of legal action and whose organization into a plaintiff class is

hindered by what has come to be known as the Tragedy of the Commons.

In an accompanying footnote, the court suggested, 500 F.Supp. at 989 n.1:

Organizing a plaintiff class is hindered by the fact that the benefit of a successful lawsuit against the polluter for compensation is not limited to the plaintiffs. Persons damaged by the pollution but not contributing to the legal action also benefit due to the collateral estoppel effects of the initial lawsuit in subsequent actions and because the first plaintiff or group of plaintiffs has already done the work of organizing some relevant evidence and locating experts willing to testify. Thus, each person damaged by the pollution has an economic incentive to let someone else bring the first lawsuit and then to take a "free ride" or at least a discount excursion to obtaining his own compensation.

The Tragedy of the Commons idea came from a story illustrating that if everyone can benefit from a commonly shared resource without taking into account the costs their activity imposes on others, people have an incentive to overuse that resource. In the context of aluminum production, the manufacturer's failure to take into account its pollution's effect on the common stream of air results in too much pollution and aluminum production relative to the allocatively efficient amount. *Orchard View Farms* prevents the polluter from treating the surrounding air and land as a commons.

The *Orchard View Farm* footnote excerpted above turns the traditional commons illustration on its head. In Hardin's example, people were ignoring external harms and overindulging in grazing. In the footnote, the plaintiffs are ignoring external benefits and underindulging in beneficial lawsuits. Each person to sue a polluter successfully creates an external benefit by assembling evidence of the polluter's activity and halting pollution that may have damaged many. Since no plaintiff producing this benefit is entitled to compensation from others he has benefitted, an underproduction of such suits is likely. Punitive damages increase the incentives.

8. The "commons" approach helps identify which externalities require federal regulation and which are addressed efficiently by state or local regulation. Since efficiency requires the internalization of externalities, the smallest appropriate geographic area over which the regulator must have jurisdiction is the area in which the external effects of the activity in question are felt.

Questions: Based on the regulation of the commons, what is the appropriate level of governmental control, from local to federal, to engage in the following activities: (1) control of water pollution in navigable waters, (2) impose zoning requirements, (3) enforce nuisance law to prevent loud parties or child pornography, (4) reduce acid rain to an efficient level, (5) protect the ozone layer? How is the analysis affected by the desirability of uniformity? Administrability? By the existence of a "national consensus" that everyone should share the same quality of life (e.g., Clean Air Act)?

4. THE PRISONER'S DILEMMA

Imagine the following scenario. You and an accomplice decide to rob a bank. Unfortunately, both of you are arrested just before entering the bank when a sharp-eyed but over-eager bank guard spots the pistols you are both carrying under your coats. You are both put in jail—in separate cells.

The U.S. Attorney offers you the following deal.

"We've got you cold for illegal possession of firearms. That's a two-year sentence right there. But I know you were planning more than just a stroll with a pistol. If I can prove you were attempting to rob that bank, you'll get fifteen years in jail."

You answer, "I never set foot in that bank, and you'll never be able to prove I intended to rob it. Two years is the most you can put me away for."

"Maybe," the U.S. Attorney replies, "and maybe not. But I've got a deal that can get you off scot-free. If you'll agree to testify against your accomplice, I promise to drop the charges against you. You'll spend no time in jail. Of course, your accomplice will get fifteen years."

"That sounds like a good deal," you say. "At least for me. There must be a catch."

"Of course," the U.S. Attorney replies. "I'm making an identical offer to your accomplice. And if you both squeal, you'll both get fifteen years—although I'll recommend five years off for each of you, in light of your cooperation."

Game theorists call this scenario "The Prisoner's Dilemma." The Prisoner's Dilemma illustrates how self-interest can lead rational individuals to pursue a course leading to mutual self-destruction, even when that destruction is perfectly foreseeable.

Consider the plight of the prisoner receiving an offer like the U.S. Attorney's. Whatever the prisoner's accomplice decides, the prisoner is better off testifying. If his accomplice remains silent and the prisoner squeals, the prisoner gets off scot-free; and if the accomplice testifies, the prisoner can still get a fifteen-year sentence reduced to ten by testifying as well.

The accomplice makes the same calculation and reaches the same conclusion. Neither party has an incentive to sacrifice himself by remaining silent. That will only create an opportunity for the other party to get an even greater benefit from squealing. Unless both prisoners can get together somehow to make a deal, they will both testify, to their mutual loss. Their self-destructive actions will be perfectly rational and perfectly foreseeable.

Notes and Questions

1. One obvious connection between the Prisoner's Dilemma and the Tragedy of the Commons is that all individuals are expected to further

their self-interest.   Rational individuals will not attempt to control the external costs they impose on others because they recognize that there is nothing to be gained by behaving responsibly.   It will not stop others from imposing costs on them.   In a world of self-interested individuals, a unilateral attempt to behave responsibly only puts the responsible party at a competitive disadvantage.   Thus, rational maximizers cannot be expected to avoid imposing external costs—externalities will not solve themselves. Prisoners seek to minimize their own punishment without regard to their confederate's interests.   Herdsmen are expected to maximize their profits without any concern for the welfare of other herdsmen or society.

Question: Assuming that the self-interested model accurately depicts how people make decisions, how can each herdsman's position be analogized to each prisoner's?

2.   A second connection among the Prisoner's Dilemma, externalities, and private property is that the Prisoner's Dilemma illustrates the potential gains when parties can find a means to control external costs.   If the two prisoners could only get together, they might be able to arrange a deal where each would refuse to testify against the other and both would receive likely sentences of two years rather than ten.   Garrett Hardin and others have suggested that one hope of controlling external costs may lie with private property.

Question: How does privatizing the common eliminate the Prisoner's Dilemma for herdsmen?

B.   ASSIGNING AND EXCHANGING RIGHTS

1.   COMPETING USES AND THE COEXISTENCE OF PROPERTY RIGHTS

Even if it is agreed that assigning private property rights may lead to an efficient allocation of resources, the question remains, to whom should such rights be assigned?   Assigning property rights involves more than determining real estate boundaries.   Property is not a patch of ground but a collection of rights to the exclusive use of resources. For example, ownership of real property may involve the right to occupy the land; the right to occupy or control the use of the airspace above the land to a particular altitude or even infinitely; the right to receive the sunlight and rain that falls on the land; the right to erect structures on the land that block light and rain from others; the right to clean air passing over the land; and the right to use air passing over the land to carry away smoke and other pollutants.   The following cases explore the criteria courts may use in deciding to whom such rights should be assigned.

BRYANT v. LEFEVER

Court of Appeals, 1879.

4 C.P.Div. 172, 48 L.J. 380, C.P.

BRAMWELL, L.J.:

The plaintiff says that he is possessed of a house, that for more than twenty years this house and its occupants have had the wind blow to, over and from it, and that he has, as so possessed, the right that it should continue to do so. That the defendants have interfered with this right and prevented the free access and departure of the wind. He adds that they have committed a nuisance to him as so possessed. He has proved that he is possessed of a house more than twenty years old, that the wind had access to it and passage over it for twenty years without the hindrance recently caused by the defendants; that the defendants have caused a hindrance by putting on the roof of their house (which is as old as the plaintiff's), timber to a considerable height, thereby preventing the wind blowing to and over the plaintiff's house when in some directions, and passing away from it when in others; that this causes his chimneys to smoke as they did not before, to the extent of being a nuisance. The question is if this shews a cause of action. First, what is the right of the occupier of a house in relation to air, independently of length of enjoyment? It is the same as that which land and its owner or occupier have, it is not greater because a house has been built. That puts no greater burthen or disability on adjoining owners. What then is the right of land and its owner or occupier? It is to have all natural incidents and advantages as nature would produce them. There is a right to all the light and heat that would come, to all the rain that would fall, to all the wind that would blow; a right that the rain which would pass over the land should not be stopped and made to fall on it, a right that the heat from the sun should not be stopped and reflected on it, a right that the wind should not be checked, but should be able to escape freely; and if it were possible that these rights were interfered with by one having no right, no doubt an action would lie. But these natural rights are subject to the right of adjoining owners, who for the benefit of the community have and must have rights in relation to that use and enjoyment of their property that qualify and interfere with those of their neighbours; right to use their property in the various ways in which property is commonly and lawfully used. A hedge, a wall, a fruit tree, would each affect the land next to which it was planted or built. They would keep off some light, some air, some heat, some rain when coming from one direction, and prevent the escape of air, of heat, of wind, of rain when coming from the other. But nobody could doubt that in such case no action would lie. Nor will it in the case of a house being built and having such consequences. That is an ordinary and lawful use of property as much so as the building of a wall or planting of a fence, or an orchard. Of course the same reasoning applies to the putting of timber on the top of a house which, if not a common, is a perfectly lawful act, and it would be absurd to suppose that the defendants could lawfully put another storey to their house with the consequences to the plaintiff of which he complains, but cannot put an equal height of timber. These are elementary and obvious considerations, but if borne in mind will assist very materially in the decision of this case.

* * *

But it is said, and the jury have found, that the defendants have done that which has caused a nuisance to the plaintiff's house. We think there is no evidence of this. No doubt there is a nuisance, but it is not of the defendants' causing. They have done nothing in causing the nuisance. Their house and their timber are harmless enough. It is the plaintiff who causes the nuisance by lighting a coal fire in a place the chimney of which is placed so near the defendants' wall that the smoke does not escape, but comes into the house. Let the plaintiff cease to light his fire; let him move his chimney; let him carry it higher, and there would be no nuisance. Who, then, causes it? It would be very clear that the plaintiff did, if he had built the house or chimney after the defendants had put the timber on their roof; and it is really the same though he did so before the timber was there. But (what is in truth the same answer) if the defendants cause the nuisance, they have a right to do so. If the plaintiff has not the right to the passage of air, except subject to the defendants' right to build or put timber on their house, then his right is subject to their right, and though a nuisance follows from the exercise of their right, they are not liable. *Sic utere tuo ut alienum no laedas* is a good maxim. But, in our opinion, the defendants do not infringe it. The plaintiff would, if he succeeded. We are of opinion that judgment should be for the defendants on the cause of action the subject of this appeal.

COASE, THE PROBLEM OF SOCIAL COST *

3 J. L. & Econ. 1, 2, 13 (1960).

This paper is concerned with those actions of business firms which have harmful effects on others. The standard example is that of a factory the smoke from which has harmful effects on those occupying neighbouring properties. The economic analysis of such a situation has usually proceeded in terms of a divergence between the private and social product of the factory * * *. The conclusions to which this kind of analysis seems to have led most economists is that it would be desirable to make the owner of the factory liable for the damage caused to those injured by the smoke, or alternatively, to place a tax on the factory owner varying with the amount of smoke produced and equivalent in money terms to the damage it would cause, or finally, to exclude the factory from residential districts (and presumably from other areas in which the emission of smoke would have harmful effects on others). It is my contention that the suggested courses of action are inappropriate * * *.

* * *

The traditional approach has tended to obscure the nature of the choice that has to be made. The question is commonly thought of as one in which A inflicts harm on B and what has to be decided is: how should we restrain A? But this is wrong. We are dealing with a problem of a reciprocal nature. To avoid the harm to B would inflict harm on A. The real question that has to be decided is: should A be allowed to harm B or should B be allowed to harm A? The problem is to avoid the more serious harm. * * *

* * *

* * * Who caused the smoke nuisance [in Bryant v. LeFever]? The answer seems fairly clear. The smoke nuisance was caused both by the man who built the wall *and* by the man who lit the fires. Given the fires, there would have been no smoke nuisance without the wall; given the wall, there would have been no smoke nuisance without the fires. Eliminate the wall *or* the fires and the smoke nuisance would disappear. [I]t is clear that *both* were responsible and *both* should be forced to include the loss of amenity due to the smoke as a cost in deciding whether to continue the activity which gives rise to the smoke. * * *

The judge's contention that it was the man who lit the fires who alone caused the smoke nuisance is true only if we assume that the wall is the given factor. This is what the judges did by deciding that the man who erected the higher wall had a legal right to do so. The case would have been even more interesting if the smoke from the chimneys had injured the timber. * * * [T]here can be little doubt that the man who lit the fires would have been liable for the ensuing damage to the timber, in spite of the fact that no damage had occurred until the high wall was built by the man who owned the timber.

Notes and Questions

1. In *Bryant,* a pollution case with a novel twist, only the person emitting the smoke suffers the harm. The factual complexity giving rise to the lawsuit is that before the neighbors added another story to their house and piled lumber on top, the wind drew the smoke up the chimney just fine. The argument that the neighbors were the *cause* of the smoke backing up in the chimney is quite appealing. If the neighbors were required to pay damages, then they would have an incentive to internalize the costs of their construction activities.

From Coase's perspective, however, both parties were engaged in activities which, when combined, resulted in damage. If there is no natural or obvious way to determine which party "causes" the harm in an incompatible uses case, the court's decision boils down to which party's use should be protected, the storage of lumber or the drafting of smoke. According to Coase, the problem is to "avoid the more serious harm"; that is, to protect the use with the greater value. Another way to phrase the question is to ask which party should internalize the costs of the activities, that is, be given an incentive to decide whether the activity should continue, cease, or be modified in some way.

Even though both the plaintiff and the defendant could take some action to minimize the cost, one party could avoid the detriment at less cost. Suppose that if the plaintiff must bear the cost of the smoking chimney, his only alternative is building his chimney higher, at a cost of

£60. If the defendant must bear the cost, he might store his timber elsewhere, which would eliminate the plaintiff's harm but result in storage fees of £20 per year. Ignoring the distributional implications, eliminating the harm for £20 is preferred. The same benefit is achieved more inexpensively by making the person who can avoid the injury at the lowest cost liable for the costs.

Realizing that sometimes one party may be better able to avoid the harms of incompatible uses has led law and economics scholars to support rules placing liability on the party who can avoid the injury at the lowest cost, the *best cost avoider*. Ronald Coase's observation that every party to the injury "causes" the injury removes the moral overtones, the aura of blameworthiness, associated with conflicting land uses and allows analysts to focus on maximizing the value of land use. The "best cost avoider" approach supplies a substitute for the "causation" approach.

2. If the plaintiff could avoid the smoke only by building a new chimney for £40 and the defendant could avoid the injury only by renting storage space for £20, the defendant is the best cost avoider. But if the defendant does not have the £20, he will be unable to rent the storage space or pay the £40 for damages. Since neither choice is viable, his only alternative is to cease storing timber. Suppose that storing wood is the defendant's occupation. Putting the defendant out of work may seem to be a harsh result if the plaintiff is wealthy enough to build a higher chimney.

Question: Could such a result possibly be economically efficient?

3. Imagine that the plaintiff could avoid the injury by maintaining a higher chimney at a cost of £60 per year and the defendant could avoid the injury only by building a separate structure to hold his timber, at the cost of £50 per year. The plaintiff's damage, if neither of these precautions is taken, is £40 per year.

Question: If the injury can only be avoided by means that are more expensive than the cost of the accident, is making the best cost avoider liable still allocatively efficient?

STURGES v. BRIDGMAN

Chancery Division, 1879.
XI C.D. 852.

THESIGER, L.J.:

The Defendant in this case is the occupier, for the purpose of his business as a confectioner, of a house in *Wigmore Street*. In the rear of the house is a kitchen, and in that kitchen there are now, and have been for over twenty years, two large mortars in which the meat and other materials of the confectionery are pounded. The Plaintiff, who is a physician, is the occupier of a house in *Wimpole Street,* which until recently had a garden at the rear, the wall of which garden was a party-wall between the Plaintiff's and the Defendant's premises, and formed the back wall of the Defendant's kitchen. The Plaintiff has, however, recently built upon the site of the garden a consulting-room, one of the side walls of which is the wall just described. It has been proved that in the case of the mortars, before and at the time of action brought, a noise was caused which seriously inconveniences the Plaintiff in the use of his consulting-room, and which, unless the Defendant had acquired a right to impose the inconvenience, would constitute an actionable nuisance. The Defendant contends that he had acquired the right * * * by uninterrupted [use] for more than twenty years.

* * * [T]he laws governing the acquisition of easements by [use] stands thus: Consent or acquiescence of the owner of the [affected land] lies at the root of prescription. * * * [A] man cannot, as a general rule, be said to consent to or acquiesce in the acquisition by his neighbour of an easement through an enjoyment of which he has no knowledge, actual or constructive, or which he contests and endeavours to interrupt, or which he temporarily licenses. It is a mere extension of the same notion, or rather it is a principle into which by strict analysis it may be resolved, to hold, that an enjoyment which a man cannot prevent raises no presumption of consent or acquiescence. * * *

It is said that if this principle is applied in cases like the present, and were carried out to its logical consequences, it would result in the most serious practical inconveniences, for a man might go—say into the midst of the tanneries of Bermondsey, or into any other locality devoted to a particular trade or manufacture of a noisy or unsavoury character, and, by building a private residence upon a vacant piece of land, put a stop to such trade or manufacture altogether. The case also is put of a blacksmith's forge built away from all habitations, but to which, in course of time, habitations approach. We do not think that either of these hypothetical cases presents any real difficulty. As regards the first, it may be answered that whether anything is a nuisance or not is a question to be determined, not merely by an abstract consideration of the thing itself, but in reference to its circumstances; what would be a nuisance in Belgrave Square would not necessarily be so in Bermondsey; and where a locality is devoted to a particular trade or manufacture carried on by the traders or manufacturers in a particular and established manner not constituting a public nuisance, Judges and juries would be justified in finding and may be trusted to find, that the trade or manufacture so carried on in that locality is not a private or actionable wrong. As regards the blacksmith's forge, that is really an *idem per item* case with the present. It would be on the one hand in a very high degree unreasonable and undesirable that there should be a right of action for acts which are not in the present condition of the adjoining land, and possibly never will be any annoyance or inconvenience to either its owner or occupier; and it would be on the other hand in an equally degree unjust, and from a public point of view, inexpedient that the use and value of the adjoining land should, for all time and under all circumstances, be restricted and diminished by reason of the continuance of acts incapable of physical interruption, and which the law gives no power to prevent. The smith in the case supposed might protect himself by taking a sufficient curtilage to ensure what he does from being at any time an annoyance to his neighbour, but the neighbour himself would be powerless in the matter. Individual cases of hardship may occur in the strict carrying out of the principle upon which we found our judgment, but the negation of the principle would lead even more to individual hardship, and would at the same time produce a prejudicial effect upon the development of land for residential purposes. The Master of the Rolls in the Court below took substantially the same view of the matter as ourselves and granted the relief which the Plaintiff prayed for, and we are of opinion that his order is right and should be affirmed * * *.

Notes and Questions

1. The confectioner in *Sturges* argued that he had acquired a right to use his noisy mortars because he had used them without interruption for more than twenty years (the period traditionally held sufficient to acquire an "easement by prescription" in England). During those years, the plaintiff-doctor had no way to know about the defendant's mortars. Therefore, the doctor was in no position either to have objected or acquiesced to their use. Without the actual or constructive knowledge necessary to challenge the use, the court holds, the presumption of acquiescence (the foundation for an easement by prescription) is untenable and no easement is granted.

Prescriptive easements have a counterpart in the law of adverse possession, which permits a person in possession of another's land to acquire not only the right to use that land but even title to that land. In either case, the use (for an easement) or possession (for title) must be "open and notorious" and the adverse use or possession must continue for a statutory time period. This ensures that the landowner will have an opportunity to detect the use or possession and its adverse character. Easements by prescription and adverse possession serve an efficiency purpose by allocating rights from an owner who is not using his land and who fails to object to another's use or possession of his land to someone using the scarce resource as an owner normally would.

A presumption underlying adverse possession is that the adverse possessor values the land more than someone not using it at all. Under an alternative theory, the person not objecting to a continuously ongoing externality of which he could reasonably have been aware suffers less harm if the adverse use continues than the adverse claimant would suffer if barred from the use or possession after so long.

Questions: Is use always valued more highly than non-use? Do the requirements that the use be open and notorious and continue for a long time period provide any protection for the landowner who values his land in its natural state?

2. Having disposed of the issue of priority in time, Lord Justice Thesiger established that whether an activity is a nuisance depends on all the circumstances, in particular, where the activity is carried out and which party was in the best position to take precautions to avoid harming those whose land uses came later (a blacksmith could, at the time of setting

up his shop, acquire sufficient surrounding land that what he does would be no annoyance to his neighbors).

Question: From the perspective of allocating resources to their most valuable uses, why are these factors relevant to whether a use is a nuisance?

3. Lord Justice Thesiger was explicitly promoting the development of cities and towns: "From a public point of view, [it would be] inexpedient that the use and value of the adjoining land should, for all time and under all circumstances be restricted and diminished by reason of the continuance of acts incapable of physical interruption." Yet he clearly was concerned with residential development even though the plaintiff in *Sturges* wanted to develop his residence to further his medical practice: "The negation of this principle would * * * produce a prejudicial effect upon the development of land for residential purposes."

From an efficiency perspective, there is no obvious reason to believe that land is generally valued more for residential than industrial or business purposes. The Lord Justice decided that residential use was more valuable but did not indicate what evidence supported his decision. Without evidence as to the value of competing uses, he relied on evidence about the neighborhood's characteristics and, inevitably, on his own values.

Questions: Is there a significant danger that the Lord Justice's closer identification with the doctor, a fellow professional, than with the confectioner, a tradesman, would affect his judgment about the relative value of their activities, about the significance of development of land for residential uses? Could class biases of this sort result in the inefficient allocation of land?

2. THE COASE THEOREM AND THE EFFICIENT EXCHANGE OF RIGHTS

In a free market with no obstacles to bargaining between the parties, voluntary exchange allocates goods to their most valuable uses. The previous section illustrated courts' attempts to wrestle with cases where the economic issue is the allocation of "costs" rather than goods. In his classic article, The Problem of Social Cost (which may have inspired the law and economics movement), Ronald Coase presented the fundamental insight that voluntary exchange not only allocates goods efficiently, but *costs* as well. Coase proposed that, as long as the parties can bargain freely, they will eventually come to an agreement that minimizes the costs or harms resulting from incompatible property uses. He noted, "It is always possible to modify by transactions in the market the initial legal delimitation of rights. And, of course, if such market transactions are costless, such a rearrangement of rights will always take place if it would lead to an increase in the value of production." That proposition, known as the *Coase Theorem,* is often stated as follows: As long as there are no obstacles to bargaining between the parties involved, resources will be allocated efficiently regardless of how property rights are initially assigned.

Coase's Theorem is a dramatic assertion because it means that, if there are no transaction costs, judges do not affect the allocative efficiency of resource use by assigning rights or liability to one party or the other. As Coase put it, "It is necessary to know whether the damaging business is liable or not for damage caused since without the establishment of this initial delimitation of rights there can be no market transactions to transfer and recombine them. But the ultimate result (which maximizes the value of production) is independent of the legal position if the pricing system is assumed to work without cost. * * * Judges have to decide on legal liability but this should not confuse economists about the nature of the economic problem involved." The excerpted opinions devote much attention to justifying their chosen assignments of rights. Coase's Theorem, however, implies that time could be saved by simply assigning rights randomly. If parties seeking conflicting land uses can bargain about which use should prevail, the party who values his use most highly will always prevail.

Consider the application of Coase's Theorem to *Fontainebleau Hotel.* Does it matter whether the law assigns a property right to cast a shadow to the Fontainebleau, or a right to sunlight to the Eden Roc?

FONTAINEBLEAU HOTEL CORP. v. FORTY–FIVE TWENTY–FIVE, INC.

District Court of Appeals of Florida, 1959.
114 So.2d 357.

PER CURIAM.

This is an interlocutory appeal from an order temporarily enjoining the appellants from continuing with the construction of a fourteen-story addition to the Fontainebleau Hotel, owned and operated by the appellants. Appellee, plaintiff below, owns the Eden Roc Hotel, which was constructed in 1955, about a year after the Fontainebleau, and adjoins the Fontainebleau on the north. Both are luxury hotels, facing the Atlantic Ocean. The proposed addition to Fontainebleau is being constructed twenty feet from its north property line, 130 feet from the mean high water mark of the Atlantic Ocean, and 76 feet 8 inches from the ocean bulkhead line. The 14–story tower will extend 160 feet above grade in height and is 416 feet long from east to west. During the winter months, from around two o'clock in the afternoon for the remainder of the day, the shadow of the addition will extend over the cabana, swimming pool, and sunbathing areas of the Eden Roc, which are located in the southern portion of its property.

* * *

The chancellor heard considerable testimony on the issues made by the complaint and the answer and, as noted, entered a temporary injunction restraining the defendants from continuing with the construction of the addition. His reason for so doing was stated by him, in a memorandum opinion, as follows:

> "In granting the temporary injunction in this case the Court wishes to make several things very clear. * * * It is based solely on the proposition that no one has a right to use his property to the injury of another. In this case it is clear from the evidence that the proposed use by the Fontainebleau will materially damage the Eden Roc. There is evidence indicating that the construction of the proposed annex by the Fontainebleau is malicious or deliberate for the purpose of injuring the Eden Roc, but it is scarcely sufficient, standing alone, to afford a basis for equitable relief."

This is indeed a novel application of the maxim *sic utere tuo ut alienum non laedas*. This maxim does not mean that one must never use his own property in such a way as to do any injury to his neighbor. It means only that one must use his property so as not to injure the lawful *rights* of another. In Reaver v. Martin Theatres, under this maxim, it was stated that "it is well settled that a property owner may put his own property to any reasonable and lawful use, so long as he does not thereby deprive the adjoining landowner of any right of enjoyment of his property *which is recognized and protected by law, and so long as his use is not such a one as the law will pronounce a nuisance*." [Emphasis supplied by this Court.]

No American decision has been cited, and independent research has revealed none, in which it has been held that—in the absence of some contractual or statutory obligation—a landowner has a legal right to the free flow of light and air across the adjoining land of his neighbor. * * *

There being, then, no legal right to the free flow of light and air from the adjoining land, it is universally held that where a structure serves a useful and beneficial purpose, it does not give rise to a cause of action, either for damages or for an injunction under the maxim *sic utere tuo ut alienum non laedas,* even though it causes injury to another by cutting off the light and air and interfering with the view that would otherwise be available over adjoining land in its natural state, regardless of the fact that the structure may have been erected partly for spite.

We see no reason for departing from this universal rule. * * *

Since it affirmatively appears that the plaintiff has not established a cause of action against the defendants by reason of the structure here in question, the order granting a temporary injunction should be and it is hereby reversed with directions to dismiss the complaint.

Notes and Questions

1. Nowhere in its discussion of the parties' relative rights does the court in *Fontainebleau* consider whether the Eden Roc's sunny swimming pool or the Fontainebleau's 14–story addition was more valuable. Finding no precedent for giving a landowner a legal right to the flow of sunlight

across a neighbor's adjoining land, the Florida Court of Appeals resolved the issue without considering which use was more valuable. A court determined to allocate resources to their most valuable uses would have to acknowledge that sometimes the right to sunlight is valuable, especially to Miami Beach hotels.

The facts of *Fontainebleau* provide an opportunity to illustrate the Coase Theorem that, absent impediments to exchange, the court's initial allocation of the right will not affect the ultimate efficiency of resource use. The mere existence of damage to the Eden Roc does not mean that the addition to the Fontainebleau was not the more valuable use. If the addition added $1,000,000 annually to the Fontainebleau's profits while reducing the Eden Roc's profits by only $500,000 annually, then using the land for the addition increased the value of beachfront property in Miami Beach. If these values are correct, then the court reached an efficient result, without explicitly attempting to do so.

> *Questions:* If the court had come out the other way, had granted an injunction halting the construction, would the Eden Roc have enforced the injunction or would the owners of the Fontainebleau have paid the Eden Roc to allow them to build? How much would the Fontainebleau be willing to pay annually?

2. Suppose that the tower would damage the Eden Roc ($750,000 in lost profits annually) more than it would aid the Fontainebleau ($500,000 additional annual profits).

> *Questions:* If the parties could bargain freely, would the Eden Roc's owners be willing and able to pay more to stop the construction than the Fontainebleau would gain by having the construction? Would bargaining lead to an efficient allocation of resources? If the court enjoined construction under these facts, what result would the Fontainebleau's bargaining produce?

3. Reexamine Sturges v. Bridgman and Bryant v. Lefever. According to Coase, the possibility of bargaining eliminates the need for the court to find whose land use is more valuable.

> *Question:* Would bargaining have ensured that the most valuable use prevailed in each of those cases regardless of how the court ruled?

PRAH v. MARETTI

Supreme Court of Wisconsin, 1982.
108 Wis.2d 223, 321 N.W.2d 182.

ABRAHAMSON, JUSTICE.

* * *

According to the complaint, the plaintiff is the owner of a residence which was constructed during the years 1978–1979. The complaint alleges that the residence has a solar system which includes collectors on the roof to supply energy for heat and hot water and that after the plaintiff built his solar-heated house, the defendant purchased the lot adjacent to and immediately to the south of the plaintiff's lot and commenced planning construction of a home. The complaint further states that when the plaintiff learned of defendant's plans to build the house he advised the defendant that if the house were built at the proposed location, defendant's house would substantially and adversely affect the integrity of plaintiff's solar system and could cause plaintiff other damage. Nevertheless, the defendant began construction. The complaint further alleges that the plaintiff is entitled to "unrestricted use of the sun and its solar power" and demands judgment for injunctive relief and damages.

* * *

This court's reluctance in the nineteenth and early part of the twentieth century to provide broader protection for a landowner's access to sunlight was premised on three policy considerations. First, the right of landowners to use their property as they wished, as long as they did not cause physical damage to a neighbor, was jealously guarded.

Second, sunlight was valued only for aesthetic enjoyment or as illumination. Since artificial light could be used for illumination, loss of sunlight was at most a personal annoyance which was given little, if any, weight by society.

Third, society had a significant interest in not restricting or impeding land development. This court repeatedly emphasized that in the growth period of the nineteenth and early twentieth centuries change is to be expected and is essential to property and that recognition of a right to sunlight would hinder property development. * * *

Considering these three policies, this court concluded that in the absence of an express agreement granting access to sunlight, a landowner's obstruction of another's access to sunlight was not actionable. These three policies are no longer fully accepted or applicable. They reflect factual circumstances and social priorities that are now obsolete.

First, society has increasingly regulated the use of land by the landowner for the general welfare.

Second, access to sunlight has taken on a new significance in recent years. In this case the plaintiff seeks to protect access to sunlight, not for aesthetic reasons or as a source of illumination but as a source of energy. Access to sunlight as an energy source is of significance both to the landowner who invests in solar collectors and to a society which has an interest in developing alternative sources of energy.

Third, the policy of favoring unhindered private development in an expanding economy is no longer in harmony with the realities of our society. The need for easy and rapid development is not as great today as it once was, while our perception of the value of sunlight as a source of energy has increased significantly.

Courts should not implement obsolete policies that have lost their vigor over the course of the years. The law of private nuisance is better suited to resolve landowners' disputes about property development in the 1980's than is a rigid rule which does not recognize a landowner's interest in access to sunlight. * * *

* * *

* * * Recognition of a nuisance claim for unreasonable obstruction of access to sunlight will not prevent land development or unduly hinder the use of adjoining land. It will promote the reasonable use and enjoyment of land in a manner suitable to the 1980's. That obstruction of access to light might be found to constitute a nuisance in certain circumstances does not mean that it will be or must be found to constitute a nuisance under all circumstances. The result in each case depends on whether the conduct complained of is unreasonable.

Accordingly we hold that the plaintiff in this case has stated a claim under which relief can be granted.

Notes and Questions

1. Assuming that there are no impediments to bargaining between Prah and Maretti, the Coase Theorem states that bargaining will inevitably produce an efficient allocation of sunlight, whether to Maretti's house or to Prah's solar collectors. The failure to halt construction of the hotel addition in *Fontainebleau* meant that the plaintiff would have to take the initiative in bargaining with the defendant. It might appear that the only consequence of the Wisconsin Supreme Court recognizing that blocking sunlight could be a nuisance in *Prah* is that in Wisconsin the defendant would have to take the initiative in bargaining with the plaintiff. Ronald Coase believed that: "[W]ithout the establishment of [an] initial delimitation of rights there can be no market transactions to transfer and recombine them." In other words, the courts' only role is to ensure that rights are clearly assigned to *someone*. If the initial allocation is clear, the parties are in a position to discuss a reallocation.

Question: Justice Abrahamson apparently believed that recognizing a right to sunlight would promote the development of alternative energy sources. If the Coase Theorem is correct can Justice Abrahamson also be correct?

2. *The Invariance Hypothesis:* According to the Coase Theorem, if building the new home is worth more to the Marettis than the sunlight is worth to Prah, the new home will be built so long as the Marettis have enough funds to bribe Prah into allowing it. If sunlight is more valuable to Prah than the new construction is to the Marettis, the Marettis will not build their home so long as Prah has sufficient funds to bribe them not to. The court's decision is irrelevant to the efficient allocation of resources and what the court does appears to have no effect on the property's ultimate use. In other words, rights will end up with the party willing to pay the most for them, and the court's original allocation of right has no effect on that willingness to pay.

This interpretation of the Coase Theorem is referred to as the "Invariance Hypothesis" or the "Strong Version" of the Coase Theorem. The Invariance Hypothesis posits that as long as no obstacles to transactions exist between affected parties, the allocation of resources will be efficient *and* that efficient allocation of resources will be the same regardless of how property rights are initially assigned.

The Invariance Hypothesis is derived from an example involving a cattle raiser and a neighboring farmer developed by Coase to explain his theory. To simplify Coase's example somewhat, assume that the cattle raiser's cow is worth $5 and can be expected to stray and damage $10 of the farmer's crops. To appreciate the possibility that the allocation of resources does not depend on the rights assignment, consider three allocation questions:

a. Will the rights assignment affect whether the rancher keeps the cow? If the rancher has the right to let her cow trample the farmer's crops, the farmer has an incentive to offer the rancher a payment in return for the rancher getting rid of the cow. The farmer would pay up to $10 to avoid the damage from the cow. This is more than the cow is worth, so a rational rancher is likely to allow herself to be bribed, for some amount between $5 and $10, to get rid of the cow. But if the rancher does not have the right to trample the farmer's crops, the rancher will also get rid of the cow, preferring to get rid of a $5 cow rather than pay $10 for the damage it causes.

b. Will the rights assignment affect whether a fence is built to contain the cow? Perhaps the cow could be prevented from trampling the crops by building a fence between the two properties. Assume that the cost of the fence would be $3. If the rancher has the right to let her cow trample the farmer's crop, the farmer will build the $3 fence—this is cheaper than either suffering $10 in crop damage, or giving the rancher a bribe between $5 and $10 to get rid of the cow. And once again, if the rancher does not have the right to trample the farmer's crops, the rancher will build the fence. A $3 fence is cheaper than either paying $10 in damages or getting rid of a $5 cow. Either way, the fence gets built.

c. Will the rights assignment affect whether the farmer plants crops? Suppose that the cow destroyed crops worth $10, but which cost $8 to grow. If the rancher has the right to let her cow trample the farmer's crops, the farmer will stop growing crops altogether. The farmer is unwilling to pay more than $2—the net value of the destroyed crops—as a bribe to the rancher, and the rancher will not accept such a small amount to get rid of a $5 cow. Similarly, if the rancher does not have the right to trample the farmer's crops, the rancher will pay the farmer a bribe not to plant. After all, if the crops are planted the rancher will either have to pay $10 in damages or get rid of a $5 cow; it is less expensive to pay the farmer a bribe between $2 and $5 not to plant. Once again, whether the right is assigned to the farmer or the rancher, no crops are planted.

Part of the symmetry in outcomes is explained by the fact that the potential for exchange appears to internalize otherwise-external costs completely. For the rancher, the damage done by the cow is a cost whether she has to compensate the farmer for his loss, or simply give up the opportunity to get a payment from the farmer by keeping the cow. Similarly, if the farmer has the right to exclude the cow, excluding it is a cost because he gives up the opportunity to get a payment. If the farmer does not have the right, then excluding the cow costs him the amount of the payment he must make. The assignment of rights determines who receives and who pays bribes, but the allocation of resources to crops, cattle, and fences does not vary.

Coase's version of these hypothetical situations is only slightly more complicated. He assumed that the increased crop damage as the herd got larger was as shown below:

Size of Herd (No. of Cows)	Annual Crop Loss (in dollars)
1	1
2	3
3	6
4	10

If the cattle raiser has the right to trample the farmer's crop, the farmer has an incentive to bargain with her to keep the size of the herd relatively small. The farmer is willing to pay an amount equal to the damage done by a cow to prevent the cattle raiser from increasing her herd size. Thus, the farmer would pay up to one dollar to avoid the damage from the first cow, two dollars (the *additional* damage done) to prevent the herd from increasing from one to two cows, three dollars (the *additional* damage done by adding the third cow) to prevent the herd from expanding from two cows to three, and four dollars (the *additional* damage done by adding the fourth cow) to prevent expansion from three to four. The cattle raiser will decide how large a herd to have depending on the bribe the farmer is willing to pay and how much each cow is worth in the market for beef. If each cow is worth enough, no bribe that the farmer is willing to pay will reduce the herd size, but if each cow is worth $3.50 as beef, then the cattle raiser would rather take a bribe greater than $3.50 not to add the cow to her herd. Since the farmer is willing to pay an amount up to four dollars, the bribe is likely to occur if there are no obstacles to bargaining.

If the cattle raiser has no right to trample the farmer's crops, the cattle raiser has an incentive to bargain with the farmer to allow her cattle to trample. The cattle raiser is willing to pay an amount no greater than the value of each cow to have trampling rights. Once again, if each cow is worth $3.50, the cattle raiser will have a herd of three, because she will not be able to strike a bargain for rights to the fourth, which would add an additional four dollars in crop loss to the farmer, more than that cow is worth to the cattle raiser.

3. Limitations on the Invariance Hypothesis: Those challenging the Invariance Hypothesis generally focus on the conclusion that the allocation of resources is unaffected by the assignment of rights rather than the conclusion that the allocation will be efficient. The most obvious problem with the Invariance Hypothesis involves the parties' relative willingness and ability to buy rights. The initial assignment of rights *does* affect the parties' relative wealth. Since a party's willingness and ability to pay are affected by wealth, the assignment of a right to one party may determine the outcome in terms of the actual uses to which resources are put.

To understand the wealth effects of the rights assignment, consider how a rancher's valuation of her pet dog depends on how rights are assigned. Suppose that the rancher's dog can be expected to stray and kill $10 of a neighboring farmer's chickens. The dog could be restrained with a $3 fence. If the rancher had the right to let her dog roam free, the farmer would be willing to build the $3 fence to avoid the $10 in lost chickens. But if the rancher must pay for the dog's damage, and if the rancher is too poor to build a $3 fence—the dog must go. Implicit in the farmer's willingness to build the fence is the assumption that the rancher was unwilling to accept less than $3 to get rid of the dog. If the rancher must pay for the damage, however, and is poor, the rancher may not be willing and able to pay $3 to build the fence. The result in both cases is efficient. However, the initial allocation of the rights, by affecting the parties' willingness and ability to pay, has changed which outcome is efficient. The rancher valued the dog at more than $3 when assigned the right to let it roam free, so building a $3 fence made economic sense to the farmer. When forced to pay for its damage, the rancher valued the dog at less than $3, so building a $3 fence did not make economic sense to her.

The limitations of the Invariance Hypothesis have led many economists to adopt the version of the Coase Theorem with which this section started: As long as there are no obstacles to transactions between affected parties, the resources will be allocated efficiently regardless of how property rights are initially assigned.

Questions: The discussion of the invariance of the allocative efficiency that would result from bargaining in *Prah* in Question 2 above included two qualifications: "so long as the Marettis have enough funds to bribe Prah" and "so long as Prah has sufficient funds to bribe the Marettis." How is the wealth of Prah and the Marettis affected by the assignment of rights? Might the distribution of wealth affect whether the residence gets built or whether the solar collectors continue to receive sunlight?

4. *Partial Equilibrium Analysis:* If the use of solar collectors is widespread, recognizing the right to bring a nuisance action for blocking sunlight will have effects beyond parties to the suit and beyond bargains between future adjacent landowners whose uses conflict. Among those effects is a decrease in the value of undeveloped land located near homes with solar collectors. The use to which such land can be put is diminished by recognizing the right and so the land's value is diminished; the portions of the land on which large homes can be built are limited. Recognizing the right will also affect the market for undeveloped land and will have corresponding distributional effects, benefitting those who already have already built homes and harming those who would like to develop property. Those effects are externalities, harms and benefits resulting from the assignment of rights that are not taken into account in the process of assigning the right.

When determining whether a reallocation is efficient, economists frequently ignore external effects, such as price changes in a market other than the one under consideration, and wealth redistribution effects. These effects may be significant. Analysis focuses on the allocation of resources in a single market after bargaining has taken place, when the market is in *equilibrium*. Economists often ignore distributional effects or effects on the allocation of other resources, referring to them as secondary or "second order" effects. Examining effects in one market at a time simplifies analysis that otherwise would be too complicated. Sometimes it is necessary to focus on just part of a question, do a *partial* analysis, in order to gain any useful answer at all. Recognizing that the analysis of a single market in equilibrium is only part of the larger picture, economists describe such analysis as *partial equilibrium analysis*.

The analysis of each of the cases thus far has been partial equilibrium analysis that ignores many effects of property rights assignments on wealth distribution and on markets for other resources. While partial equilibrium analysis is useful, many apparently efficient bargains between individuals have effects other than those considered in the partial analysis.

5. *General Equilibrium Analysis:* An assignment of rights has effects that ripple out beyond a single market. A *general equilibrium analysis* considers the wealth effects of a property rights assignment in numerous markets. Even if changes in the parties' wealth resulting from being assigned or denied the property right are not sufficiently large to influence the final allocation of the resource in question, those changes still affect the parties' purchasing habits in two ways. First, since a wealth transfer between parties occurred, the winner now has command over resources that formerly the loser commanded. If the winner and loser spend their money differently, the allocation of other resources shifts in favor of those the winner values. The allocation is still efficient, but who is valuing those uses has changed. If winner and loser have different values, different preferences, the allocation of resources will change.

In addition, the winner's increase in wealth may alter the winner's preferences. Wealthy people are more likely to acquire yachts than are poor people. A poor person must satisfy her nautical desires by renting rowboats. As an individual becomes wealthier, she may be willing and able to devote more resources to luxuries than to basics. The winner's demand for fine wine increases while her demand for jug wine decreases. The loser's altered preferences may exactly compensate for the changes in the winner's tastes, but an exact match is extremely unlikely.

Thus, from both general and partial equilibrium perspectives, the ultimate allocations of resources resulting from alternative property rights assignments will all be efficient (assuming there are no transaction costs) but the allocations may be different.

6. Reexamine Sturges v. Bridgman and Bryant v. Lefever in light of the Coase Theorem, recognizing the limitations of the Invariance Hypothesis. The possibility of bargaining eliminates the need for the court to find who is the best cost avoider of the injuries. Whoever is assigned liability for injuries caused by the conflicting land use will negotiate with the other to find who could avoid the injury at least cost and then pay that person (if it is the other party) to take the appropriate precautions. Where bargaining is possible, the bargaining rather than the court determines the best cost avoider of the injury.

Questions: Would bargaining have ensured that the most valuable use prevailed in each of those cases regardless of how the court ruled? Assume that the plaintiff in *Bryant*, the owner of the fireplace, was poor. Would his ultimate ability to use the fireplace depend on whether he was granted the injunction? Would the character of the ultimate use have been invariant regardless of how the court ruled?

BOOKER v. OLD DOMINION LAND CO.

Supreme Court of Appeals of Virginia, 1948.
188 Va. 143, 49 S.E.2d 314.

BUCHANAN, JUSTICE.

* * *

In 1937, Old Dominion Land Company subdivided about 114 acres of its land, lying north of Newport News, in Warwick county, into lots, named the subdivision Parkview and made a map thereof, which was recorded. There were about 164 of these lots, laid off along and abutting on the east and west sides of what was called Jefferson avenue on the map, and which is now U.S. Highway No. 168. The company thereupon proceeded to sell these lots and at the time of the institution of this suit had sold all of them. Twelve of the lots were marked "business" and a few as "sold" or "reserved," and the rest were for residential purposes. The deeds for the residential lots contained identical restrictions [restricting their development to dwelling houses costing not less than $1,500.00 each and prohibiting commercial uses of the land until January 1, 1959.]

* * *

Plaintiffs are the owners of [two lots] in this subdivision, conveyed to them June 13, 1946, by deed reciting that it was subject to the restrictions, covenants and conditions contained in the original deeds from the Old Dominion Land Company.

The ground alleged by the plaintiffs as entitling them to a cancellation of the restrictions is a change of conditions "so radical as to destroy the essential objective and purposes of the covenants, conditions and restrictions originally contained in the Old Dominion Land Company deeds.

* * *

The former sales manager [for Old Dominion] testified that the lots were sold by the map; when the lots marked "business" were sold, it was represented to the purchasers that the lots not so marked could be used only for residences, and that the company received a higher price for the business lots because of the residential restrictions. By the same token, he testified, the values of the lots designated as residential were enhanced by the residential restrictions.

Thus it would occur that elimination of these restrictions would result in taking away a value bought and paid for by the owners of both business and residential properties, and in many instances without so much as a "by-your-leave," because many of the owners are not before the court.

* * *

* * * [I]n a building development plan the creation of an area restricted to residences contemplates the continued existence of such an area from which business is excluded. It is to prevent the anticipated encroachment of business on the protected area that the restrictions are created. Purchasers of lots in such an area buy in reliance upon the fact that all other lots in the area are subject to the same restriction, and the entire development will retain its character as a purely residential district. The very purpose of the restriction is to prevent the property from being converted to business use if it should become more valuable for that use.

* * * The relief here sought, if granted, would nullify the covenants, at least in plaintiff's title, for all time and all purposes even though future changes might completely remove the ground for doing so. More is required to warrant such a decree * * *. It must be established that the whole plan has become inoperative and that its objects can no longer be carried out.

The decree [denying the relief sought] is

Affirmed.

Notes and Questions

1. The materials in this section explore the efficiency implications of bargaining between parties to impose limits on each other's use of their property. Courts often must decide whether to enforce these restrictions once the parties have agreed upon them. That decision will also involve an allocative choice. In *Booker*, Judge Buchanan stated "The very purpose of the restriction is to prevent the property from being converted to business use if it should become more valuable for that use." He makes it sound like the restriction is designed to prevent allocative efficiency and then upholds the restriction.

Question: Is the restriction's purpose to prevent property from going to its most valuable use and, if so, are such restrictions inherently inefficient?

2. Judge Buchanan referred to evidence that the real estate developer received a higher price for both the business lots and the residential lots because of the residential restrictions. This means that the development as a whole is more valuable with the restrictions than without and that the restrictive covenants enhance the allocative efficiency of the use of this resource. Judge Buchanan was concerned that elimination of these restrictions would result in taking away a value bought and paid for by both business and residential property owners.

Question: Why would any buyer of either business or residential land be willing to pay more for restricted use land?

3.   If purchasers are willing to pay more for land where restrictions on use ensure that the externalities some uses create do not occur, then for a court to lift the restrictions or refuse to enforce the contractual restrictions appears inefficient.   Judge Buchanan held that "It must be established that the whole plan has become inoperative and that its objects can no longer be carried out" before the restrictions would be removed.

Questions: Is this test consistent with the underlying efficiency rationale for such restrictions?   When should these restrictions be removed?

4.   A similar restrictive covenant was discussed in Mountain Springs Ass'n of N.J., Inc. v. Wilson, 81 N.J.Super. 564, 196 A.2d 270 (1963).   In *Mountain Springs,* the court voided terms of the covenant restricting property owners' rights to sell to people who were not members of the association because the restriction was unlimited in duration, unreasonable in the limitation of the number of permitted purchasers, and granted the association too much power to control prospective purchasers.   It is sometimes argued that the price of land in such a community reflects the nature of the restrictions imposed on the land and that some buyers will be willing and able to pay more for stricter limitations.   Voiding terms of a restrictive covenant must therefore be inefficient, since it substitutes a lower-valued (unrestricted) use for a higher-valued (restricted) use.   Each of the three grounds for voiding the covenant in *Mountain Springs,* however, suggests a set of restrictions unnecessarily broad to achieve the purposes of the covenant.

Questions: If the terms of a restrictive covenant are more restrictive than necessary to achieve the desired purpose, will the price of the land necessarily be higher than if the restrictions were more precisely drafted?   Who bears the cost of an unnecessarily restrictive covenant, the members of the association or society as a whole?

5.   While the previous cases have explored the efficiency implications of private agreements resolving conflicting land uses, *Booker* presents questions involved in the enforcement of such agreements.

Questions: If all of the parties to an agreement wished to remove the restrictive covenant, then would removing the restriction be a Pareto superior reallocation and allocatively efficient?   If a group of people can agree privately to restrict their property to residential use, should the court enforce the restriction until private negotiations produce agreement on eliminating the restrictions?

C.   TRANSACTION COSTS AND IMPEDIMENTS TO BARGAINING

1.   THE COASE THEOREM AND TRANSACTION COSTS

The Coase Theorem states that as long as there are no obstacles to transactions between affected parties, bargaining will ensure an efficient allocation of resources regardless of how property rights are initially assigned.   The key to appreciating the Coase Theorem is understanding the implications of the assumption that there are no obstacles to transactions between affected parties. The following cases examine when obstacles to bargaining arise, the efficiency implications of those transaction costs, and legal mechanisms for promoting allocative efficiency when transaction costs are substantial.

PLOOF v. PUTNAM

Supreme Court of Vermont, 1908.
81 Vt. 471, 71 A. 188.

MUNSON, J.

It is alleged as the ground of recovery that on the 13th day of November, 1904, the defendant was the owner of a certain island in Lake Champlain, and of a certain dock attached thereto, which island and dock were then in charge of the defendant's servant; that the plaintiff was then possessed of and sailing upon said lake a certain loaded sloop, on which were the plaintiff and his wife and two minor children; that there then arose a sudden and violent tempest, whereby the sloop and the property and persons therein were placed in great danger of destruction; that, to save these from destruction, or injury, the plaintiff was compelled to, and did, moor the sloop to defendant's dock; that the defendant, by his servant, unmoored the sloop, whereupon it was driven upon the shore by the tempest, without the plaintiff's fault; and that the sloop and its contents were thereby destroyed, and the plaintiff and his wife and children cast into the lake and upon the shore, receiving injuries. This claim is set forth in two counts * * * charging that the defendant by his servant * * * willingly and designedly unmoored the sloop [and] alleging that it was the duty of the defendant by his servant to permit the plaintiff to moor his sloop to the dock, and to permit it to remain so moored during the continuance of the tempest, but that the defendant by his servant, in disregard of this duty, negligently, carelessly, and wrongfully unmoored the sloop. [The defendant objected to both claims on the grounds that he had the right to eject trespassers from his property.]

There are many cases in the books which hold that necessity, as an inability to control movements inaugurated in the proper exercise of a strict right, will justify entries upon land and interferences with personal property that would otherwise have been trespasses. * * *

This doctrine of necessity applies with special force to the preservation of human life. One assaulted and in peril of his life may run through the close of another to escape from his assailant. One may sacrifice the personal property of another to save his life or the lives of his fellows. * * *

It is clear that an entry upon the land of another may be justified by necessity, and that the declaration before us discloses a necessity for mooring the sloop. But the defendant questions the sufficiency of the counts because they do not negative the existence of natural objects to which the plaintiff could have moored with equal safety. The allegations are, in substance, that the stress of a sudden and violent tempest compelled the plaintiff to moor to defendant's dock to save his sloop and the people on it. The averment of necessity is complete, for it covers not only the necessity of mooring, but the necessity of mooring to the dock * * * .

[The judgment of the trial court denying the defendant's motion for summary judgment on the grounds that the allegations were insufficient to state a cause of action was affirmed.]

Notes and Questions

1. *Ploof* presents another case of conflicting uses of resources—in this instance, the defendant's dock. Mr. Putnam, through his servant, was protecting his right to exclusive possession of the land and dock. The plaintiff, Mr. Ploof, valued the dock as a means of preventing harm to his family and boat. Property owners like Mr. Putnam are normally protected against interference with their right to exclusive possession by the law of trespass. Under the doctrine of trespass by necessity, however, Mr. Ploof's intrusion is not only allowed but protected; Ploof was awarded damages because his sloop was unmoored from defendant Putnam's dock. The court permitted the plaintiff to use the dock, in furtherance of a public policy valuing human life more than the right to exclusive possession of property.

Applying the private necessity doctrine involved the court in the question of which party's use of the dock is more valuable. As the Coase Theorem suggests, it may have been necessary for the law to assign the right to one of the parties so that they would have a reference point for bargaining about departures from that assignment of rights. This does not explain why the law should recognize a private necessity defense.

Questions: If the defendant has a right to exclusive possession, would bargaining between the parties lead to an efficient outcome? What are the transaction costs in private necessity cases generally?

2. To arrange a mutually beneficial exchange of rights, parties must become aware of the potential gains of exchange, identify the other party with whom they hope to exchange, establish communication with that party, negotiate the terms of the exchange, and then perform the exchange. At each stage, impediments may arise and costs may be incurred.

When discussing the court's opinion in *Sturges,* Coase argued that "[i]t was of course the view of the judges that they were affecting the working of the economic system—and in a desirable direction. * * * The judges' view that they were settling how the land was to be used would be true only in the case in which the costs of carrying out the necessary market transactions exceeded the gains which might be achieved by any rearrangement of rights." Coase recognized that sometimes the costs of bargaining to reallocate rights exceed the efficiency benefits of reallocation. In such a case, the least expensive course of action is to suffer the inefficiency, unless rights can be redefined to facilitate bargaining or an efficient outcome.

In reality, market transactions almost always involve some costs, and sometimes substantial ones. In many factual circumstances like the one in

Ploof, transaction costs prevent the efficient reallocation of rights through bargaining and the initial allocation of rights made by the court may be the final allocation. In such cases, the court's decision matters very much to the efficient allocation of resources.

3. If transaction costs prevent bargaining from allocating resources efficiently, then substitutes for bargaining may maximize societal welfare. One substitute might be legal rules that permit a party who values a resource more highly to take that resource from its owner and pay damages. Another alternative would employ a court or other decisionmaker to allocate the resource directly to those who (the decisionmaker believes) value the resource most highly and forbid bargaining over reallocations. In the following excerpt, Calabresi and Melamed describe rules requiring bargaining before rights can be exchanged as *property rules*. The alternatives are characterized as *liability rules* and *inalienability rules,* respectively. The discussion of Vincent v. Lake Erie Transport Co., which follows the excerpt from Calabresi and Melamed, employs that nomenclature in evaluating the efficiency implications of the private necessity doctrine introduced in *Ploof.*

CALABRESI AND MELAMED, PROPERTY RULES, LIABILITY RULES, AND INALIENABILITY: ONE VIEW OF THE CATHEDRAL *
85 Harv.L.Rev. 1089, 1092–93, 1105 (1972).

Only rarely are Property and Torts approached from a unified perspective. Recent writings by lawyers concerned with economics and by economists concerned with law suggest, however, that an attempt at integrating the various legal relationships treated by these subjects would be useful both for the beginning student and the sophisticated scholar. By articulating a concept of "entitlements" which are protected by property, liability, or inalienability rules, we present one framework for such an approach. * * *

* * *

An entitlement is protected by a property rule to the extent that someone who wishes to remove the entitlement from its holder must buy it from him in a voluntary transaction in which the value of the entitlement is agreed upon by the seller. * * *

Whenever someone may destroy the entitlement if he is willing to pay an objectively determined value for it, the entitlement is protected by a liability rule. This value may be what it is thought the original holder of the entitlement would have sold it for. But the holder's complaint that he would have demanded more will not avail him once the objectively determined value is set. * * *

An entitlement is inalienable to the extent that its transfer is not permitted between a willing buyer and a willing seller. * * *

It should be clear that most entitlements to most goods are mixed. Taney's house may be protected by a property rule in situations in which Marshall wishes to purchase it, by a liability rule where the government decides to take it by eminent domain, and by a rule of inalienability in situations where Taney is drunk or incompetent. * * *

* * *

Whenever society chooses an initial entitlement it must also determine whether to protect the entitlement by property rules, by liability rules, or by rules of inalienability. In our framework, much of what is generally called private property can be viewed as an entitlement protected by a property rule. No one can take the entitlement to private property from the holder unless the holder sells it willingly and at the price at which he subjectively values the property. Yet a nuisance with sufficient public utility to avoid an injunction has, in effect, the right to take property with compensation. In such a circumstance the entitlement to the property is protected only by what we call a liability rule: an external, objective standard of value used to facilitate the transfer of the entitlement from the holder to the nuisance. Finally, in some instances we will not allow the sale of the property at all, that is, we will occasionally make the entitlement inalienable.

VINCENT v. LAKE ERIE TRANSPORT CO.

Supreme Court of Minnesota, 1910.
109 Minn. 456, 124 N.W. 221.

O'BRIEN, J.

The steamship Reynolds, owned by the defendant, was for the purpose of discharging her cargo on November 27, 1905, moored to plaintiff's dock in Duluth. While the unloading of the boat was taking place a storm from the northeast developed, which at about 10 o'clock p.m., when the unloading was completed, had so grown in violence that the wind was then moving at 50 miles per hour and continued to increase during the night. There is some evidence that one, and perhaps two, boats were able to enter the harbor that night, but it is plain that navigation was practically suspended from the hour mentioned until the morning of the 29th, when the storm abated, and during that time no master would have been justified in attempting to navigate his vessel, if he could avoid doing so. After the discharge of the cargo the Reynolds signaled for a tug to tow her from the dock, but none could be obtained because of the severity of the storm. If the lines holding the ship to the dock had been cast off, she would doubtless have drifted away; but, instead, the lines were kept fast, and as soon as one parted or chafed it was replaced, sometimes with a larger one. The vessel lay upon the outside of the dock, her bow to the east, the wind and waves striking her starboard quarter with such force that she was constantly being lifted and thrown against the dock, resulting in its damage, as found by the jury, to the amount of $500.

We are satisfied that the character of the storm was such that it would have been highly imprudent for the master of the Reynolds to have attempted to leave the dock or to have permitted his vessel to drift a way from it. * * *

The appellant contends * * * that, because its conduct during the storm was rendered necessary by prudence and good seamanship under conditions over which it had no control, it cannot be held liable for any injury resulting to the property of others, and claims that the jury should have been so instructed. An analysis of the charge given by the trial court is not necessary, as in our opinion the only question for the jury was the amount of damages which the plaintiffs were entitled to recover, and no complaint is made upon that score.

The situation was one in which the ordinary rules regulating property rights were suspended by forces beyond human control, and if, without the direct intervention of some act by the one sought to be held liable, the property of another was injured, such injury must be attributed to the act of God, and not to the wrongful act of the person sought to be charged. If during the storm the Reynolds had entered the harbor, and while there had become disabled and been thrown against the plaintiffs' dock, the plaintiffs could not have recovered. Again, if while attempting to hold fast to the dock the lines had parted, without any negligence, and the vessel carried against some other boat or dock in the harbor, there would be no liability upon her owner. But here those in charge of the vessel deliberately and by their direct efforts held her in such a position that the damage to the dock resulted, and, having thus preserved the ship at the expense of the dock, it seems to us that her owners are responsible to the dock owners to the extent of the injury inflicted.

* * *

Theologians hold that a starving man may, without moral guilt, take what is necessary to sustain life; but it could hardly be said that the obligation would not be upon such person to pay the value of the property so taken when he became able to do so. And so public necessity, in times of war or peace, may require the taking of private property for public purposes; but under our system of jurisprudence compensation must be made.

Let us imagine in this case that for the better mooring of the vessel those in charge of her had appropriated a valuable cable lying upon the dock. No matter how justifiable such appropriation might have been, it would not be claimed that, because of the overwhelming necessity of the situation, the owner of the cable could not recover its value.

This is not a case where life or property was menaced by any object or thing belonging to the plaintiff, the destruction of which became necessary to prevent the threatened disaster. Nor is it a case where, because of the act of God, or unavoidable accident, the infliction of the injury was beyond the control of the defendant, but is one where the defendant prudently and advisedly availed itself of the plaintiffs' property for the purpose of preserving its own more valuable property, and the plaintiffs are entitled to compensation for the injury done.

Order affirmed.

LEWIS, J.

I dissent. It was assumed on the trial before the lower court that appellant's liability depended on whether the master of the ship might, in the exercise of reasonable care, have sought a place of safety before the storm made it impossible to leave the dock. The majority opinion assumes that the evidence is conclusive that appellant moored its boat at respondent's dock pursuant to contract, and that the vessel was lawfully in position at the time the additional cables were fastened to the dock, and the reasoning of the opinion is that, because appellant made use of the stronger cables to hold the boat in position, it became liable under the rule that it had voluntarily made use of the property of another for the purpose of saving its own.

In my judgment, if the boat was lawfully in position at the time the storm broke, and the master could not, in the exercise of due care, have left that position without subjecting his vessel to the hazards of the storm, then the damage to the dock, caused by the pounding of the boat, was the result of an inevitable accident. If the master was in the exercise of due care, he was not at fault. The reasoning of the opinion admits that if the ropes, or cables, first attached to the dock had not parted, or if, in the first instance, the master had used the stronger cables, there would be no liability. If the master could not, in the exercise of reasonable care, have anticipated the severity of the storm and sought a place of safety before it became impossible, why should he be required to anticipate the severity of the storm, and, in the first instance, use the stronger cables?

I am of the opinion that one who constructs a dock to the navigable line of waters, and enters into contractual relations with the owner of a vessel to moor at the same, takes the risk of damage to his dock by a boat caught there by a storm, which event could not have been avoided in the exercise of due care, and further, that the legal status of the parties in such a case is not changed by renewal of cables to keep the boat from being cast adrift at the mercy of the tempest.

Notes and Questions

1. *Vincent* establishes that the right to trespass on another's property in a private emergency does not include the right to cause physical damage to the property. According to the majority, the ship owner is liable for damages if he acted to save his own property at the expense of another's, regardless of whether it was prudent. Using the terminology of Calabresi and Melamed, in an emergency, the dock owner's right to the dock was protected by a liability rule rather than a property rule. If protected by a property rule, the dock owner would be entitled to forbid any boat from using his dock during a storm. A boat in distress would have to bargain with the dock owner. If protected by a liability rule, the dock owner would

not be entitled to forbid any boat owner from tying up at his dock during a storm but would be able to collect from the boat owner any damages to the dock caused by the boat's presence.

> *Questions:* What would it mean to assign the right to the boat owner and protect it by a property or liability rule? What kind of rule was adopted in *Ploof?* To whom was the right assigned and how was it protected in *Vincent?* Are the legal rules in *Ploof* and *Vincent* inconsistent?

2. If no obstacles to bargaining existed between the parties in *Vincent,* the party with the greater willingness and ability to pay to protect his property could exclude the other party. If bargaining cannot occur and there is no obligation to pay damages, one party would be able to impose external costs on the other.

> *Questions:* Given the factual circumstances, was there any reason to protect the dock owner's right by a liability rule rather than a property rule? Are the incentives created for the boat owners by making them pay damages likely to lead to an efficient result? In these factual circumstances, are the incentives created by a liability rule more likely to give an efficient result than those created by the property rule?

3. *Vincent* illustrates how, when substantial impediments to bargaining exist between the parties, liability rules may be superior to property rules as a means of internalizing costs that would otherwise be external to one of the decisionmakers. Having decided on a liability rule rather than a property rule, it still must be decided who should be liable to whom. If the dock owner bears the costs of incompatible uses, he will be forced to choose between suffering injury to his dock or setting the boat adrift and risking liability under the rule in *Ploof.* Alternatively, if the boat owner bears the costs of incompatible uses, the boat owner (or captain) must choose between the risks of letting the boat drift and liability for damage to the dock under *Vincent.*

> *Question:* Are the two parties in equivalent positions to evaluate the risk or is one party in the better position to evaluate the risks and act so as to minimize the risk?

4. In his dissent, Justice Lewis argued that the situation in *Vincent* differed from the usual emergency because the parties had a contractual relationship. That suggests that they had an opportunity to negotiate the allocation of the risks presented by potential emergencies. He believed that the risk of dock damage was part of the dock owner's cost of doing business.

> *Question:* Should the contractual relationship between the parties make any difference to the assignment of liability in this case?

2. IMPEDIMENTS TO BARGAINING AND THE CHOICE OF REMEDIES

The *Ploof* and *Vincent* cases deal with trespass, a one-time invasion of another's property right to exclusive use of a resource. In the ordinary trespass, the parties have little opportunity to bargain. The trespasser may not have anticipated the trespass, and the person whose resource is invaded frequently is not even present for bargaining when the trespass occurs. Nuisance cases that involve a chronic, continuing invasion of another's right present different problems. The fundamental inquiry, however, is still whether there is any reason why, when one person's enjoyment of her resource is disturbed on a continuing basis by another's noise, vibration, or pollution, the parties cannot get together and bargain themselves into an efficient outcome. The following cases explore various transaction costs that may prevent allocative efficiency and raise questions about the efficiency of alternative remedies available to courts.

BOOMER v. ATLANTIC CEMENT COMPANY

Court of Appeals of New York, 1970.
26 N.Y.2d 219, 309 N.Y.S.2d 312, 257 N.E.2d 870.

BERGAN, JUDGE.

Defendant operates a large cement plant near Albany. These are actions for injunction and damages by neighboring land owners alleging injury to property from dirt, smoke and vibration emanating from the plant. A nuisance has been found after trial, temporary damages have been allowed; but an injunction has been denied. * * *

* * *

* * * The total damage to plaintiffs' properties is * * * relatively small in comparison with the value of defendant's operation and with the consequences of the injunction which plaintiffs seek.

The ground for the denial of injunction, notwithstanding the finding both that there is a nuisance and that plaintiffs have been damaged substantially, is the large disparity in economic consequences of the nuisance and of the injunction. This theory cannot, however, be sustained without overruling a doctrine which has been consistently reaffirmed in several leading cases in this court and which has never been disavowed here, namely that where a nuisance has been found and where there has been any substantial damage shown by the party complaining an injunction will be granted.

* * *

Although the court at Special Term and the Appellate Division held that injunction should be denied, it was found that plaintiffs had been damaged in various specific amounts up to the time of the trial and damages to the respective plaintiffs were awarded for those amounts. * * *

The court at Special Term also found the amount of permanent damage attributable to each plaintiff, for the guidance of the parties in the event both sides stipulated to the payment and acceptance of such permanent damage as a settlement of all the controversies among the parties.   The total of permanent damages to all plaintiffs thus found was $185,000.   * * *

This result at Special Term and at the Appellate Division is a departure from a rule that has become settled; but to follow the rule literally in these cases would be to close down the plant at once. This court is fully agreed to avoid that immediately drastic remedy; the difference in view is how best to avoid it. [The defendant's investment in the plant is in excess of $45,000,000.   There are over 300 people employed there.]

One alternative is to grant the injunction but postpone its effect to a specified future date to give opportunity for technical advances to permit defendant to eliminate the nuisance; another is to grant the injunction conditioned on the payment of permanent damages to plaintiffs which would compensate them for the total economic loss to their property present and future caused by defendant's operations.   For reasons which will be developed the court chooses the latter alternative.

* * *

[T]echniques to eliminate dust and other annoying by-products of cement making are unlikely to be developed by any research the defendant can undertake within any short period, but will depend on the total resources of the cement industry nationwide and throughout the world. The problem is universal wherever cement is made.

For obvious reasons the rate of the research is beyond control of defendant. If at the end of 18 months the whole industry has not found a technical solution a court would be hard put to close down this one cement plant if due regard be given to equitable principles.

On the other hand, to grant the injunction unless defendant pays plaintiffs such permanent damages as may be fixed by the court seems to do justice between the contending parties. All of the attributions of economic loss to the properties on which plaintiffs' complaints are based will have been redressed.

* * *

It seems reasonable to think that the risk of being required to pay permanent damages to injured property owners by cement plant owners would itself be a reasonable effective spur to research for improved techniques to minimize nuisance.

* * *

Thus it seems fair to both sides to grant permanent damages to plaintiffs which will terminate this private litigation.   * * *

The judgment, by allowance of permanent damages imposing a servitude on land, which is the basis of the actions, would preclude future recovery by plaintiffs or their grantees.

* * *

The orders should be reversed, without costs, and the cases remitted to Supreme Court, Albany County to grant an injunction which shall be vacated upon payment by defendant of such amounts of permanent damage to the respective plaintiffs as shall for this purpose be determined by the court.

JASEN, JUDGE, dissenting.

* * *

It has long been the rule in this State, as the majority acknowledges, that a nuisance which results in substantial continuing damage to neighbors must be enjoined. To now change the rule to permit the cement company to continue polluting the air indefinitely upon the payment of permanent damages is, in my opinion, compounding the magnitude of a very serious problem in our State and Nation today.

The harmful nature and widespread occurrence of air pollution have been extensively documented. Congressional hearings have revealed that air pollution causes substantial property damage, as well as being a contributing factor to a rising incidence of lung cancer, emphysema, bronchitis and asthma.

* * *

I see grave dangers in overruling our long-established rule of granting an injunction where a nuisance results in substantial continuing damage. In permitting the injunction to become inoperative upon the payment of permanent damages, the majority is, in effect, licensing a continuing wrong. It is the same as saying to the cement company, you may continue to do harm to your neighbors so long as you pay a fee for it. Furthermore, once such permanent damages are assessed and paid, the incentive to alleviate the wrong would be eliminated, thereby continuing air pollution of an area without abatement.

* * *

This kind of inverse condemnation may not be invoked by a private person or corporation for private gain or advantage. Inverse condemnation should only be permitted when the public is primarily served in the taking or impairment of property. The promotion of the interests of the polluting cement company has, in my opinion, no public use or benefit.

* * *

I would enjoin the defendant cement company from continuing the discharge of dust particles upon its neighbors' properties unless, within 18 months, the cement company abated this nuisance.

* * *

Notes and Questions

1. Prior to *Boomer*, New York law recognized a right to injunction whenever a nuisance imposed significant costs on the plaintiff, without regard to any offsetting benefits from the nuisance-causing activity. Judge

Bergan's opinion for the majority focused on the wastefulness of shutting down the defendant's $45 million plant just to avoid $185,000 in damages to the eight plaintiffs involved in this suit. Rather than shut down the plant, the injunction was conditioned upon the payment of damages. In effect, the plaintiff's property right to be free of the polluting nuisance was transformed into a liability right to receive compensation for the injuries caused by the nuisance.

According to the Coase Theorem, if there are no impediments to bargaining between the homeowners and the cement plant, the parties will bargain their way to the efficient allocation no matter where the court initially assigns the right. The Coase Theorem focuses attention on the efficiency justification for a judicial decision that allows a resource, formerly protected by a property right, to be protected now only by a liability right. Suppose the cement plant was worth $45 million as an ongoing business but would be worthless if shut down.

Questions: If an injunction had been issued as dissenting Judge Jasen wished, what is the maximum the cement plant's owners would offer to avoid being shut down? What is the minimum the homeowners would demand to allow it to continue operating? Could transaction costs have prevented the plant's owners from successfully bargaining with the plaintiffs to refrain from enforcing the injunction?

2. Because the injunctive remedy is the traditional relief accorded in nuisance cases, courts often focus on a balancing of harms and benefits from shutting down the polluter. For instance, in Koseris v. J.R. Simplot Co., 82 Idaho 263, 352 P.2d 235, 237 (1960), the court found the following evidence relevant to its analysis of whether operation of the defendant's fertilizer plant created a nuisance:

That in the operation of its fertilizer plant it carries on a leading industry in southeastern Idaho, with a capital investment of approximately $5,500,000; that its investment in inventory at the fertilizer plant in Power County as of November 1, 1957, was $1,627,207; that as of the same date its investment at the Gay Mine * * * exceeded $1,644,000; that payments to local businesses amounted to $1,030,000; that its other purchases and sales exceeded $8,500,000; that for the year 1956 it paid over $130,000 in taxes; that nearly 1,000 employees and their dependents rely for their livelihood upon the operations of the Simplot plant, and that it has an annual payroll of more than $1,242,000.

That it had spent $223,688.00 for a fume and dust control system which constituted only a part of the total moneys expended in its attempts to control dust and fumes; that only 0.1% of any dust which is emitted from its plant due to its operations is discharged from its stacks.

The plaintiff's injured property contained only an abandoned night-club, which had been closed in 1951 under order of the sheriff and had been vacant until the time of trial except for the storage of small items. The trial court enjoined continued operation of the plant. The Idaho Supreme Court reversed on appeal, relying on the following policy argument from York v. Stallings, 217 Or. 13, 341 P.2d 529, 534 (1959), where the Supreme Court of Oregon said:

This court heretofore has accepted the balancing doctrine in cases involving the public convenience. In Fraser v. City of Portland, this court stated: "* * * sometimes a court of equity will decline to raise its restraining arm and refuse to issue an injunction * * * even though an admitted legal right has been violated, when it appears that * * * the issuance of an injunction would cause serious public inconvenience or loss without a correspondingly great advantage to the complainant."

The balancing test applied by the Idaho Supreme Court in *Koseris* appears to encourage judges to reassign property rights to pollute, or to be free from pollution, to the user who values the right most highly (see *Ploof*). If Judge Bergan was certain the economic benefits of cement production outweighed the harms, he could simply have refused to grant an injunction.

Questions: What is the justification for awarding damages in *Boomer?* What are the risks of awarding damages instead of granting an injunction? Consider dissenting Judge Jasen's point that pollution not only causes property damage, but also is "a contributing factor to a rising incidence of lung cancer, emphysema, bronchitis and asthma."

3. The previous questions have developed the rationale for selecting a liability rule over a property rule in nuisance cases but have not addressed whether the cement plant or the homeowners should be given the incentive to investigate ways to reduce the costs of pollution.

Questions: Is there any efficiency reason to provide this incentive to one party rather than the other in *Boomer?* Does the permanent damages solution provide incentives for finding ways to reduce future pollution?

SPUR INDUSTRIES, INC. v. DEL E. WEBB DEVELOPMENT CO.

Supreme Court of Arizona, In Banc., 1972.
108 Ariz. 178, 494 P.2d 700.

CAMERON, VICE CHIEF JUSTICE.

From a judgment permanently enjoining the defendant, Spur Industries, Inc., from operating a cattle feedlot near the plaintiff Del E. Webb Development Company's Sun City, Spur appeals. * * *

* * *

In 1956, Spur's predecessors in interest, H. Marion Welborn and the Northside Hay Mill and Trading Company, developed feed-lots, about 1/2 mile south of Olive Avenue, in an area between the confluence of the usually dry Agua Fria and New Rivers. The area is well suited for cattle feeding and in 1959, there were 25 cattle feeding pens or dairy operations within a 7 mile radius of the location developed by Spur's predecessors. In April and May of 1959, the Northside Hay Mill was feeding between 6,000 and 7,000 head of cattle and Welborn approximately 1,500 head on a combined area of 35 acres.

In May of 1959, Del Webb began to plan the development of an urban area to be known as Sun City. For this purpose, the Marinette and the Santa Fe Ranches, some 20,000 acres of farmland, were purchased for $15,000,000 or $750.00 per acre. This price was considerably less than the price of land located near the urban area of Phoenix, and along with the success of Youngtown[, a retirement community nearby,] was a factor influencing the decision to purchase the property in question.

* * *

Accompanied by an extensive advertising campaign, homes were first offered by Del Webb in January 1960 and the first unit to be completed was south of Grand Avenue and approximately 2 1/2 miles north of Spur. By 2 May 1960, there were 450 to 500 houses completed or under construction. At this time, Del Webb did not consider odors from the Spur feed pens a problem and Del Webb continued to develop in a southerly direction, until sales resistance became so great that the parcels were difficult if not impossible to sell. * * *

By December 1967, Del Webb's property had extended south to Olive Avenue and Spur was within 500 feet of Olive Avenue to the north. Del Webb filed its original complaint alleging that in excess of 1,300 lots in the southwest portion were unfit for development for sale as residential lots because of the operation of the Spur feedlot.

Del Webb's suit complained that the Spur feeding operation was a public nuisance because of the flies and the odor which were drifting or being blown by the prevailing south to north wind over the southern portion of Sun City. At the time of the suit, Spur was feeding between 20,000 and 30,000 head of cattle, and the facts amply support the finding of the trial court that the feed pens had become a nuisance to the people who resided in the southern part of Del Webb's development. * * *

* * *

It is clear that as to the citizens of Sun City, the operation of Spur's feedlot was both a public and a private nuisance. They could have successfully maintained an action to abate the nuisance. Del Webb, having shown a special injury in the loss of sales, had a standing to bring suit to enjoin the nuisance. The judgment of the trial court permanently enjoining the operation of the feedlot is affirmed.

* * *

In addition to protecting the public interest, however, courts of equity are concerned with protecting the operator of a lawful, albeit noxious, business from the result of a knowing and willful encroachment by others near his business.

In the so-called "coming to the nuisance" cases, the courts have held that the residential landowner may not have relief if he knowingly came into a neighborhood reserved for industrial or agricultural endeavors and has been damaged thereby. * * *

* * *

There was no indication in the instant case at the time Spur and its predecessors located in western Maricopa County that a new city would spring up, full-blown, alongside the feeding operation and that the developer of that city would ask the court to order Spur to move because of the new city. Spur is required to move not because of any wrongdoing on the part of Spur, but because of a proper and legitimate regard of the courts for the rights and interests of the public.

Del Webb, on the other hand, is entitled to the relief prayed for (a permanent injunction), not because Webb is blameless, but because of the damage to the people who have been encouraged to purchase homes in Sun City. It does not equitable or legally follow, however, that Webb, being entitled to the injunction, is then free of any liability to Spur if Webb has in fact been the cause of the damage Spur has sustained. It does not seem harsh to require a developer, who has taken advantage of the lesser land values in a rural area as well as the availability of large tracts of land on which to build and develop a new town or city in the area, to indemnify those who are forced to leave as a result.

Having brought people to the nuisance to the foreseeable detriment of Spur, Webb must indemnify Spur for a reasonable amount of the cost of moving or shutting down. * * *

It is therefore the decision of this court that the matter be remanded to the trial court for a hearing upon the damages sustained by the defendant Spur as a reasonably foreseeable and direct result of the granting of the permanent injunction. * * *

Notes and Questions

1. Instead of awarding damages to the land developer who suffered from the nuisance of the feedlot or simply enjoining the feedlot, the court in *Spur* awarded damages to the feedlot company, to compensate it for the expense of moving to a new location. The result has appealing distributional consequences, since the feedlot was doing business in its remote location for years before the Del E. Webb Development Co. decided to develop the area, and to require it to bear the costs of moving seems unfair.

Question: Is there any efficiency justification for requiring the plaintiff to pay damages in *Spur?*

2. At first, it might appear that the court in *Spur* assigned the right to receive damages to the wrong party. Certainly Spur would appear to be the party in the best position to control the insects and odors emanating from its feedlot, perhaps through use of pesticides or chlorophyll-impregnated feeds. Del Webb, however, could best evaluate whether it was worthwhile continuing to expand his residential community southward. If the concept of best cost avoider is interpreted a little more broadly, the efficient assignment of liability would consider whether one party is in the best position to avoid a conflict over uses at all, as well as whether one party can best reduce the costs of conflict.

Question: Does this interpretation of *best cost avoider* assist in choosing whether to impose liability on Spur or Del Webb?

3. Property rules may fail to allocate resources to their most valuable uses when transaction costs prevent bargaining from transferring a resource from a lower to a higher-valuing user. In such cases, damages determined by a factfinder act as a surrogate for voluntary exchanges between the parties. Rights protected by liability rules, however, also may fail to allocate resources efficiently where there is reason to doubt the judge's or jury's determination of value (i.e, the calculation of damages).

Impediments to bargaining may occasionally be greater in one direction of reallocation between parties than in the other. For example, suppose an injunction had been granted in *Boomer* and the cement plant found itself having to negotiate with the homeowners to purchase the right to pollute. If even one homeowner held out and refused to sell, the plant would have to shut down. If the injunction were denied, however, the homeowners would have to pay the cement plant to either stop production or to develop pollution control devices. If a few homeowners refused to contribute in the hope of "freeriding" on the others' efforts, the cement plant and the remaining homeowners might still reach a mutually satisfactory agreement. Because it is more difficult for the cement plant to bribe the homeowners than vice versa, a court might prefer to award a property right to the cement plant and refuse to enter the injunction.

Similar considerations may influence a court trying to decide which of two parties making competing claims for a resource should pay damages to the other. Calculating one party's damages may be more difficult than calculating the other's. In such a case, a court may wish to allocate the liability right so as to minimize the chance of an inefficient outcome due to inaccurate damage calculations.

Questions: In Spur, which damage calculation was more reliable: Spur's claim to expenses incurred in moving the feedlot, or the homeowners' claims for losses due to the insects and odors emanating from the feedlot? How might this affect the court's decision as to which party should be required to pay damages?

4. A private nuisance, as in *Boomer,* interferes with a person's use and enjoyment of his property. While the cement particles falling on the plaintiffs' property may have dirtied their lawns, shrubs, and windows, and made their tennis courts slippery, the nuisance is private because it affected the use and enjoyment of their land. In *Spur* the nuisance of the flies and stenches was both private and public. A public nuisance interferes with a right common to the public, such as health, safety, and convenience, and need not be associated with possession of land. In *Spur,* the flies and stenches affected the use and enjoyment of the land Del Webb was developing and presented a health risk. The effect of a public nuisance is often more intangible, harder to quantify than a private nuisance's effect on the value of land.

Question: Should the fact that public nuisances often involve more intangible harms affect the choice of efficient remedies between injunction and damages?

CARPENTER v. DOUBLE R CATTLE COMPANY, INC.

Court of Appeals of Idaho, 1983.
105 Idaho 320, 669 P.2d 643.

BURNETT, JUDGE.

* * *

This lawsuit was filed by a group of homeowners who alleged that expansion of a nearby cattle feedlot had created a nuisance. The homeowners claimed that operation of the expanded feedlot had caused noxious odors, air and water pollution, noise and pests in the area. The homeowners sought damages and injunctive relief. The issues of damages and injunctive relief were combined in a single trial, conducted before a jury. Apparently it was contemplated that the jury would perform a fact-finding function in determining whether a nuisance existed and whether the homeowners were entitled to damages, but would perform an advisory function on the question of injunctive relief. The district judge gave the jury a unified set of instructions embracing all of these functions. The jury returned a verdict simply finding that no nuisance existed. The court entered judgment for the feedlot proprietors, denying the homeowners any damages or injunctive relief. This appeal followed. For reasons appearing below, we vacate the judgment and remand the case for a new trial.

The homeowners contend that the jury received improper instructions on criteria for determining the existence of a nuisance. The jury was told to weigh the alleged injury to the homeowners against the "social value" of the feedlot, and to consider "the interests of the community as a whole," in determining whether a nuisance existed.
* * *

* * *

The Second Restatement [of Torts] treats such an "intentional" invasion as a nuisance if it is "unreasonable." Section 826 of the Second Restatement now provides two sets of criteria for determining whether this type of nuisance exists:

An intentional invasion of another's interest in the use and enjoyment of land is unreasonable if

(a) the gravity of the harm outweighs the utility of the actor's conduct, or

(b) the harm caused by the conduct is serious and the financial burden of compensating for this and similar harm to others would not make the continuation of the conduct not feasible.

The present version of § 826, unlike its counterpart in the First Restatement, recognizes that liability for damages caused by a nuisance may exist regardless of whether the utility of the offending activity exceeds the gravity of the harm it has created. This fundamental proposition now permeates the entire Second Restatement. The commentary to § 822, which distinguishes between "intentional" and "unintentional" invasions, and which serves as the gateway for all succeeding sections, emphasizes that the test for existence of a nuisance no longer depends solely upon the balance between the gravity of harm and utility of the conduct. Comment d to § 822 states that, for the purpose of determining liability for damages, an invasion may be regarded as unreasonable even though the utility of the conduct is great and the amount of harm is relatively small. Comment g to the same section reemphasizes that damages are appropriate where the harm from the invasion is greater than a party should be required to bear, "at least without compensation."

* * *

Both the Second Restatement and [this Court's opinion in] *Koseris [v. J.R. Simplot]* recognize that utility of the activity alleged to be a nuisance is a proper factor to consider in the context of injunctive relief; but that damages may be awarded regardless of utility. Evidence of utility does not constitute a defense against recovery of damages where the harm is serious and compensation is feasible. Were the law otherwise, a large enterprise, important to the local economy, would have a lesser duty to compensate its neighbors for invasion of their rights than would a smaller business deemed less essential to the community. In our view, this is not, and should not be, the law in Idaho.

* * *

However, our view is not based simply upon general notions of fairness; it is also grounded in economics. The Second Restatement deals effectively with the problem of "externalities" identified in the [proceedings of the American Law Institute (ALI), which drafted the Second Restatement]. Where an enterprise externalizes some burdens upon its neighbors, without compensation, our market system does not reflect the true cost of products or services provided by that enterprise. Externalities distort the price signals essential to the proper functioning of the market.

This problem affects two fundamental objectives of the economic system. The first objective, commonly called "efficiency" in economic theory, is to promote the greatest aggregate surplus of benefits over the costs of economic activity. The second objective, usually termed "equity" or "distributive justice," is to allocate these benefits and costs in accordance with prevailing societal values. The market system best serves the goal of efficiency when prices reflect true costs; and the goal of distributive justice is best achieved when benefits are explicitly identified to the correlative costs.

Although the problem of externalities affects both goals of efficiency and distributive justice, these objectives are conceptually different and may imply different solutions to a given problem. In theory, if there were no societal goal other than efficiency, and if there were no impediments to exchanges of property or property rights, individuals pursuing their economic self-interests might reach the most efficient allocation of costs and benefits by means of exchange, without direction by the courts. However, the real world is not free from impediments to exchanges, and our economic system operates within the constraints of a society which is also concerned with distributive justice. Thus, the courts often are the battlegrounds upon which campaigns for efficiency and distributive justice are waged.

Our historical survey of nuisance law has reflected the differing emphasis upon efficiency and distributive justice. As noted, the English system of property law placed a preeminent value upon property rights. It was thus primarily concerned with distributive justice in accord with those rights. For that reason the English system favored the injunction as a remedy for a nuisance, regardless of disparate economic consequences. However, when the concept of nuisance was incorporated into American law, it encountered a different value system. Respect for property rights came to be tempered by the tort-related concept of fault, and the demands of a developing nation placed greater emphasis upon the economic objective of efficiency relative to the objective of distributive justice. The injunction fell into disfavor. The reaction against the injunction, as embodied in the First Restatement, so narrowed the concept of nuisance itself that it rendered the courts impotent to deal with externalities generated by enterprises of great utility. This reaction was excessive; neither efficiency nor distributive justice has been well served.

In order to address the problem of externalities, the remedies of damages and injunctive relief must be carefully chosen to accommodate the often competing goals of efficiency and distributive justice. *Koseris* and the Second Restatement recognize the complementary functions of injunctions and damages. Section 826(a) of the Second Restatement allows both injunctions and damages to be employed where the harm created by an economic activity exceeds its utility. Section 826(b) allows the more limited remedy of damages alone to be employed where it would not be appropriate to enjoin the activity but the activity is imposing harm upon its neighbors so substantial that they cannot reasonably be expected to bear it without compensation.

* * *

Each of the parties in the present case has viewed the Second Restatement with some apprehension. We now turn to those concerns.

The homeowners, echoing an argument made during the ALI proceedings, have contended that the test of nuisance set forth in § 826 grants large enterprises a form of private eminent domain. They evidently fear that if the utility of a large enterprise exceeds the gravity of the harm it creates—insulating it from an injunction and subjecting it to liability only in damages—the enterprise might interfere at will with the enjoyment and use of neighboring property, upon penalty only of paying compensation from time to time. Such a result might be consistent with the economic goal of efficiency, but it may conflict with the goal of distributive justice insofar as it violates a basic societal value which opposes forced exchanges of property rights.

Even those legal scholars who advocate the most limited role for injunctions as a remedy against nuisances acknowledge that damages may be inadequate, and injunctions may be necessary, where the harm in question relates to personal health and safety, or to one's fundamental freedom of action within the boundaries of his own property. Ordinarily, plaintiffs in such cases would prevail on the test which balances utility against gravity of the harm. Moreover, in the exceptional cases, the offending activity might be modified or eliminated through legislative or administrative controls such as environmental protection laws or zoning. Therefore, we expect that few cases would remain in need of a judicial remedy. However, we do not today close the door on the possibility that an injunction might lie, to protect personal healt˺ and safety or fundamental freedoms, in cases missed by the balancing test and by non-judicial controls. To this extent, our adoption of the Second Restatement's test of nuisance stops short of being absolute.

* * *

We conclude that the entire judgment of the district court, entered upon the verdict of a jury which had been improperly instructed, must be vacated. The case must be remanded for a new trial to determine whether a nuisance exists under the full criteria set forth in § 826 of the Second Restatement.

* * *

Notes and Questions

The trend in modern nuisance law has been to recognize a variety of alternative remedies for nuisance that combine both injunctive and damages components. While damages are typically the only available remedy for injuries already suffered by a plaintiff, the courts may deal with complaints of future harms by four variations of the remedies of damages or injunction:

(1) granting the plaintiff an injunction, which halts the defendant's activity if the plaintiff enforces it;

(2) awarding the plaintiff damages, which requires the defendant to compensate the plaintiff for future harm if the activity continues;

(3) denying the plaintiff an injunction, which allows the defendant's activity to continue unless the plaintiff is willing and able to pay him to stop; or

(4) awarding the defendant damages, which requires the plaintiff to compensate the defendant if the plaintiff wishes to halt the defendant's activity.

The notes and question following the preceding cases in this section have developed reasons why each of these types of remedies might be appropriate.

When devising a systematic outline of when each type is appropriate you will want to take into account the following considerations:

(1) whether we know for certain which is the more valuable use;

(2) whether we can say which of the parties is in the best position to evaluate the costs and benefits of the activities and act accordingly;

(3) what is the magnitude of transaction costs that would interfere with correcting an incorrect assignment of rights protected by property rules;

(4) what is the magnitude of costs associated with errors in damages calculations required by liability rules;

(5) whether transaction costs or damages calculations are likely to be more of a problem for one party than another; and

(6) what distributional concerns are present.

Questions: Which of the four remedies is appropriate under the facts of *Carpenter?* Which are consistent with Judge Burnett's opinion?

3. PATERNALISM AND INALIENABLE RIGHTS

Property rules prevent the transfer of an entitlement to a valuable resource unless the holder of the entitlement agrees to relinquish it in a voluntary exchange. Liability rules allow involuntary transfers if the person taking or interfering with another's entitlement pays damages in an amount determined by a neutral factfinder. A third rule governing entitlements might prohibit transfers of the entitlement altogether. Criminal rules prohibit the sale of hallucinogenic drugs, skins of rare animal species, or oneself into slavery. Rights to drugs, pelts of endangered species, and oneself cannot be transferred; they are inalienable. The following cases and materials examine whether prohibitions on such transactions are justified by concern for allocative efficiency and the circumstances under which transactions should be prohibited altogether.

SAMPLES v. MONROE

Court of Appeals of Georgia, 1987.
183 Ga.App. 187, 358 S.E.2d 273.

McMurray, Presiding Judge.

This action arises from the unmarried cohabitation of plaintiff and defendant for a period of approximately 14 years. Following the separation of the parties defendant established a residence with another woman.

Plaintiff alleges that during the period of cohabitation (1968–1982) she provided defendant with a residence, food, utilities and "paid all the necessary living expenses" for defendant, based upon the promises of defendant that his earnings would be saved for their mutual benefit. Plaintiff further alleges that the promises and statements of defendant made at the inception and during the course of their cohabitation were intentionally made to deceive plaintiff, resulting in the unjust enrichment of defendant and causing plaintiff to suffer monetary loss and mental pain and suffering. Based on theories of contract and fraud, plaintiff seeks the value of her services rendered defendant, a recovery of one-half of defendant's savings, exemplary damages, attorney fees, and costs.

Following discovery, the superior court granted defendant's motion for summary judgment. Plaintiff appeals the grant of summary judgment in favor of defendant. *Held:*

Insofar as plaintiff's action is predicated upon contract principles, it is barred by OCGA § 13–8–1, which provides in part that: "A contract to do an immoral or illegal thing is void." Plaintiff's deposition acknowledges that sex had always been part of her relationship with defendant, that sex was a part of what she furnished defendant and that defendant probably would not have moved in with her had she indicated to him that she wasn't going to give him any sex. Plaintiff's arrangement with defendant is further illustrated by the following excerpt from her deposition: "Q. Alright. Let me see if I've got this straight now. When he moved in with you, you told him that you'd render all the services to him that a wife would render to a husband, including sex. A. Yes sir. Q. And including takin' care of him? A. Yes. Q. If in consideration for that, if he'd save his money and he'd put it into an account where you two would have a nest egg where you could retire early? A. That's right." In Georgia, sexual intercourse outside of marriage is a criminal offense. *"It is well settled that neither a court of law nor a court of equity will lend its aid to either party to a contract founded upon an illegal or immoral consideration."*

* * * [T]he uncontradicted evidence shows that plaintiff's arrangement with defendant envisioned a meretricious relationship rather than a simple agreement to share living expenses. "A contract founded upon a promise to live in the future in a meretricious state is void." * * *

* * * The trial court did not err in granting defendant's motion for summary judgment.

Judgment affirmed.

CALABRESI AND MELAMED, PROPERTY RULES, LIABILITY RULES, AND INALIENABILITY: ONE VIEW OF THE CATHEDRAL *

85 Harv.L.Rev. 1089, 1111–15 (1972).

Thus far we have focused on the questions of when society should protect an entitlement by property or liability rules. However, there remain many entitlements which involve a still greater degree of societal intervention: the law not only decides who is to own something and what price is to be paid for it if it is taken or destroyed, but also regulates its sale—by, for example, prescribing preconditions for a valid sale or forbidding a sale altogether. Although these rules of inalienability are substantially different from the property and liability rules, their use can be analyzed in terms of the same efficiency and distributional goals that underlie the use of the other two rules.

While at first glance efficiency objectives may seem undermined by limitations on the ability to engage in transactions, closer analysis suggests that there are instances, perhaps many, in which economic efficiency is more closely approximated by such limitations. This might occur when a transaction would create significant externalities—costs to third parties.

For instance, if Taney were allowed to sell his land to Chase, a polluter, he would injure his neighbor Marshall by lowering the value of Marshall's land. Conceivably, Marshall could pay Taney not to sell his land; but, because there are many injured Marshalls, freeloader and information costs make such transactions practically impossible. The state could protect the Marshalls and yet facilitate the sale of the land by giving the Marshalls an entitlement to prevent Taney's sale to Chase but only protecting the entitlement by a liability rule. It might, for instance, charge an excise tax on all sales of land to polluters equal to its estimate of the external cost to the Marshalls of the sale. But where there are so many injured Marshalls that the price required under the liability rule is likely to be high enough so that no one would be willing to pay it, then setting up the machinery for collective valuation will be wasteful. Barring the sale to polluters will be the most efficient result because it is clear that avoiding pollution is cheaper than paying its cost—including its costs to the Marshalls.

Another instance in which external costs may justify inalienability occurs when external costs do not lend themselves to collective measurement which is acceptably objective and nonarbitrary. This non-monetizability is characteristic of one category of external costs which, as a practical matter, seems frequently to lead us to rules of inalienability. Such external costs are often called moralisms.

If Taney is allowed to sell himself into slavery, or to take undue risks of becoming penniless, or to sell a kidney, Marshall may be harmed, simply because Marshall is a sensitive man who is made unhappy by seeing slaves, paupers, or persons who die because they have sold a kidney. Again Marshall could pay Taney not to sell his freedom to Chase the slaveowner; but again, because Marshall is not one but many individuals, freeloader and information costs make such transactions practically impossible. Again, it might seem that the state could intervene by objectively valuing the external cost to Marshall and requiring Chase to pay that cost. But since the external cost to Marshall does not lend itself to an acceptable objective measurement, such liability rules are not appropriate.

In the case of Taney selling land to Chase, the polluter, they were inappropriate because we *knew* that the costs to Taney and the Marshalls exceeded the benefits to Chase. Here, though we are not certain of how a cost-benefit analysis would come out, liability rules are inappropriate because any monetization is, by hypothesis, out of the question. The state must, therefore, either ignore the external costs to Marshall, or if it judges them great enough, forbid the transaction that gave rise to them by making Taney's freedom inalienable.

* * *

There are two other efficiency reasons for forbidding the sale of entitlements under certain circumstances: self paternalism and true paternalism. Examples of the first are Ulysses tying himself to the mast or individuals passing a bill of rights so that they will be prevented from yielding to momentary temptations which they deem harmful to themselves. This type of limitation is not in any real sense paternalism. It is fully consistent with Pareto efficiency criteria, based on the notion that over the mass of cases no one knows better than the individual what is best for him or her. It merely allows the individual to choose what is best in the long run rather than in the short run, even though that choice entails giving up some short run freedom of choice. Self paternalism may cause us to require certain conditions to exist before we allow a sale of an entitlement; and it may help explain many situations of inalienability, like the invalidity of contracts entered into when drunk, or under undue influence or coercion. But it probably does not fully explain even these.

True paternalism brings us a step further toward explaining such prohibitions and those of broader kinds—for example the prohibitions on a whole range of activities by minors. Paternalism is based on the notion that at least in some situations the Marshalls know better than Taney what will make Taney better off. Here we are not talking about the offense to Marshall from Taney's choosing to read pornography, or selling himself into slavery, but rather the judgment that Taney was not in the position to choose best for himself when he made the choice for erotica or servitude.

The first concept we called a moralism and is a frequent and important ground for inalienability. But it is consistent with the premises of Pareto optimality. The second, paternalism, is also an important economic efficiency reason for inalienability, but it is not consistent with the premises of Pareto optimality: the most efficient pie is no longer that which costless bargains would achieve, because a person may be better off if he is prohibited from bargaining.

Finally, just as efficiency goals sometimes dictate the use of rules of inalienability, so, of course, do distributional goals. Whether an entitlement may be sold or not often affects directly who is richer and who is poorer. Prohibiting the sale of babies makes poorer those who can cheaply produce babies and richer those who through some non-market device get free an "unwanted" baby. Prohibiting exculpatory clauses in product sales makes richer those who were injured by a product defect and poorer those who were not injured and who paid more for the product because the exculpatory clause was forbidden. Favoring the specific group that has benefited may or may not have been the reason for the prohibition on bargaining. What is important is that, regardless of the reason for barring a contract, a group did gain from the prohibition.

This should suffice to put us on guard, for it suggests that direct distributional motives may lie behind asserted nondistributional grounds for inalienability, whether they be paternalism, self paternalism, or externalities. * * * For example, we may use certain types of zoning to preserve open spaces on the grounds that the poor will be happier, though they do not know it now. And open spaces may indeed make the poor happier in the long run. But the zoning that preserves open space also makes housing in the suburbs more expensive and it may be that the whole plan is aimed at securing distributional benefits to the suburban dweller regardless of the poor's happiness.

Notes and Questions

1. Maximizing the value of the goods produced in society requires that each scarce resource go to the party willing and able to pay the highest price. Maximizing utility or wealth under the Pareto criteria requires that society pursue all exchanges or reallocations that make at least one person better off and no one worse off, in terms of utility or wealth, respectively.

Questions: From the perspective of Ms. Samples and Mr. Monroe, was the agreement to exchange Ms. Sample's sexual and other services in exchange for a one-half interest in Mr. Monroe's savings a Pareto superior exchange? Did the exchange increase the value of the resources involved, as measured by willingness to pay?

2. Throughout this book economic analysis is used to evaluate whether particular rules interfere with allocating resources to their most valuable uses. Even one unacquainted with the logic of economic efficiency would undoubtedly be able to think of (even if unwilling to accept) some policy justification for prohibiting the sale of sexual services, particularly when it takes the form of prostitution. Many such policy arguments can be described as being concerned with the external effects of prostitution on parties not immediately involved in the transaction.

Questions: What are the external costs of prostitution and who bears them? Are paternalistic interests protected by a rule making sexual services inalienable? Are those costs and interests compelling enough to outweigh the benefits to the immediate parties to the transaction?

3. Calabresi and Melamed point out that rules of inalienability have distributional as well as efficiency consequences.

Question: What are the distributional implications of a prohibition on the sale of children or of sexual services?

4. In People v. Daniel, 195 Cal.App.3d 623, 241 Cal.Rptr. 3 (1987), the court denied the defendant the right (a property right) to sell his child to adoptive parents.

Questions: What efficiency justifications support the court's conclusion that this right should be inalienable? How do these efficiency justifications compare to the moral justifications for prohibiting the sale of children?

5. Imagine a community so poor in other resources that all its members found it acceptable to sell their babies to eager buyers in the neighboring wealthy community. All exchanges were voluntary and the babies had the opportunity to grow up in a family with bounteous material resources. Some members of the wealthy community, however, might object to the buying and selling of babies because they are deeply offended by treating babies as property and believe that a market for babies demeans the humanity of not only the babies but those who engage in the transactions. They may believe, contrary to the beliefs of the parties to the transactions, that engaging in the buying and selling is so bad for the participants' morals and standards that the participants are always worse off as a result of the transaction and pass criminal rules to prohibit the transactions.

Questions: Is such a paternalistic rule inconsistent with Pareto optimality? Allocative efficiency?

4. CREATING NEW ENTITLEMENTS: PROPERTY, LIABILITY, OR INALIENABILITY?

Protecting an entitlement to a resource with a property rule encourages the efficient reallocation of the resource through voluntary exchange so long as there are no substantial impediments to bargaining between parties. Where transactions costs are high, liability rules can encourage efficient reallocations when court-ordered damages act as a surrogate for exchange. A rule of inalienability may be appropriate where it prevents costs to third parties, serves paternalistic interests, or has desirable distributional consequences.

When a resource becomes sufficiently scarce to subject it to competing claims, the state resolving those claims must decide whether to protect the claimants' interests with a property, liability, or inalienability rule. In addition, the state must decide to whom the right should be allocated. A court deciding to whom a resource should be allocated may consider: (1) who values the resource most highly, and so would be the most efficient user; (2) who is in the best position to calculate the costs and benefits of using the resource and to act to minimize costs and maximize benefits; and (3) whether transactions costs or inaccurate damages are a greater risk if the right is assigned to one party than to the other.

The following case deals with the evolution of a new form of entitlement. In reading it, consider what form of rule should be used to protect the entitlement—property, liability, or inalienability? To whom should the entitlement be granted?

MOORE v. REGENTS OF THE UNIVERSITY OF CALIFORNIA

Court of Appeal, Second Division, California, 1988.
215 Cal.App.3d 709, 249 Cal.Rptr. 494.

ROTHMAN, ASSOCIATE JUSTICE.

This appeal raises fundamental questions concerning a patient's right to the control of his or her own body, and whether the commercial exploitation of a patient's cells by medical care providers, without the patient's consent, gives rise to an action for damages. This appears to be a case of first impression.

In 1976, plaintiff and appellant sought medical treatment at the Medical Center of the University of California, Los Angeles (UCLA), for a condition known as hairy-cell leukemia. He was seen by Dr. David W. Golde, who confirmed the diagnosis. As a necessary part of the treatment for this disease, plaintiff's spleen was removed at UCLA in October of 1976.

Without plaintiff's knowledge or consent, Dr. Golde and Shirley G. Quan, a UCLA employee, determined that plaintiff's cells were unique. Through the science of genetic engineering, these defendants developed a cell-line from plaintiff's cells which is capable of producing pharmaceutical products of enormous therapeutic and commercial value. The Regents, Golde and Quan patented the cell-line along with methods of producing many products therefrom. In addition, these defendants entered into a series of commercial agreements for rights to the cell-line and its products with Sandoz Pharmaceuticals Corporation (Sandoz) and Genetics Institute, Inc. (Genetics). The market potential of products from plaintiff's cell-line was predicted to be approximately three billion dollars by 1990. Hundreds of thousands of dollars have already been paid under these agreements to the developers. Without informing plaintiff, and in pursuit of their research efforts, Golde and UCLA continued to monitor him and take tissue samples from him for almost seven years following the removal of his spleen.

* * *

In deciding whether plaintiff can state a cause of action for conversion on the facts set forth in his complaint, it is necessary to review the requirements of conversion.

Conversion is "a distinct act of dominion wrongfully exerted over another's personal property in denial of or inconsistent with his title or rights therein, ... without the owner's consent and without lawful justification." It is " 'an act of wilful interference with a chattel, done without lawful justification, by which any person entitled thereto is deprived of use and possession.' "

For conversion, a plaintiff need only allege: "(1) plaintiffs' ownership or right to possession of the property at the time of the conversion; (2) defendants' conversion by a wrongful act or disposition of plaintiffs' property rights; and (3) damages."

* * *

The complaint alleges that plaintiff's tissues, including his spleen, blood, and the cell-line derived from his cells "are his tangible personal property." This is the crux of plaintiff's case for conversion.

* * *

We have approached this issue with caution. The evolution of civilization from slavery to freedom, from regarding people as chattels to recognition of the individual dignity of each person, necessitates prudence in attributing the qualities of property to human tissue. There is, however, a dramatic difference between having property rights in one's own body and being the property of another. To our knowledge, no public policy has ever been articulated, nor is there any statutory authority, against a property interest in one's own body. We are not called on to determine whether use of human tissue or body parts ought to be "gift based" or subject to a "free market." That question of policy must be determined by the Legislature. In the instant case, the cell-line has already been commercialized by defendants. We are presented a fait accompli, leaving only the question of who shares in the proceeds.

* * *

In our evaluation of the law of property, we consider the definition of the word "property" [and] find nothing which negates, and much which supports, the conclusion that plaintiff had a property interest in his genetic material.

"As a matter of legal definition, 'property' refers not to a particular material object but to the right and interest or domination rightfully obtained over such object, with the unrestricted right to its use, enjoyment and disposition. In other words, [in] its strict legal sense 'property' signifies that dominion or indefinite right of user, control, and disposition which one may lawfully exercise over particular things or objects; thus 'property' is nothing more than a collection of rights."

* * *

Plaintiff's spleen, which contained certain cells, was something over which plaintiff enjoyed the unrestricted right to use, control and disposition.

The rights of dominion over one's own body, and the interests one has therein, are recognized in many cases. These rights and interests are so akin to property interests that it would be a subterfuge to call them something else.

* * *

We are told that if plaintiff is permitted to have decisionmaking authority and a financial interest in the cell-line, he would then have the unlimited power to inhibit medical research that could potentially benefit humanity. He could conceivably go from institution to institution seeking the highest bid, and if dissatisfied, "would claim the right simply to prohibit the research entirely."

We concede that, if informed, a patient might refuse to participate in a research program. We would give the patient that right. As to defendants' concern that a patient might seek the greatest economic gain for his participation, this argument is unpersuasive because it fails to explain why defendants, who patented plaintiff's cell-line and are benefiting financially from it, are any more to be trusted with these momentous decisions than the person whose cells are being used. It has been suggested by writers that biotechnology is no longer a purely research oriented field in which the primary incentives are academic or for the betterment of humanity. Biological materials no longer pass freely to all scientists. As here, the rush to patent for exclusive use is rampant. The links being established between academics and industry to profitize biological specimens are a subject of great concern. If this science has become science for profit, then we fail to see any justification for excluding the patient from participation in those profits.

* * *

The judgments of dismissal are reversed with directions to the trial court to take proceedings consistent with the views set forth in the foregoing opinion.

* * *

GEORGE, ASSOCIATE JUSTICE.

I dissent.

* * *

I am greatly concerned about the full implications of the majority's ruling that body fluids and parts constitute a form of property. There are those who believe " 'society will benefit ... from a market in body parts'.... More body parts would be available for recipients, and donors would gain a means to make money." "Some people are revolted by the thought of a woman selling her aborted fetus. Others think it is only fair." (Sherman, *The Selling of Body Parts*, (1987) National L.J. 1.)

Plaintiff himself admits, in his third amended complaint, that had he been aware of the commercial potential of his diseased spleen he "would have considered whether to avail himself of medical, surgical and health care services at other facilities and institutions, where his wishes in this regard would have been inquired into, respected, and carried out. [P]laintiff would have sought to participate in the economic and financial benefit defendants ... are likely to receive, as a result of their research and commercial activities...."

The absence of legislation regulating the trafficking in human body parts (except where transplantation is involved) raises the specter of thriving "used body parts" establishments emulating their automotive counterparts, but not subject to regulation comparable to that governing the latter trade.

I believe we are not authorized, and should not be inclined, to create new rights and remedies in an area which so clearly lies outside the bounds of the legislatively defined cause of action for conversion and is so unsuited to judicial intervention.

* * *

Various "arguments against recognition of property rights" in human bodily substances are listed in Hardiman, *Toward the Right of Commerciality,* [34 UCLA L.Rev. 207,] 236–237 [1987]. They warrant recitation, not because I feel we are in a position to adopt or reject these arguments, but because they illustrate the complexity of the issues before us and the superiority of the Legislature's fact-finding capabilities over our own in resolving these questions: "Although compelling arguments support recognizing property rights in human tissue, arguments against recognition may also be raised. These arguments include: the potential for adverse effects on organ donation for transplantation usage; the moral aversion to treating the body as a commodity; the effect of patient hold-outs and higher transaction costs on research and tissue availability; and the threat of improper motivation in the area of tissue acquisition....

"Several potentially persuasive arguments against property rights arise in the context of organ transplantation. Opponents of organ sales predict a variety of adverse effects should a market in human organs arise: decreases in the number of organs charitably donated; increases in the number of inferior organs; competitive bidding between patients for limited resources; financial pressure on the poor to sell their organs; and unacceptable risks of death for a pecuniary profit. Without question, any adverse effects of property rights on the organ donation system are of critical importance to the health of the populace. If these rights seriously interfere with the availability of life-saving transplantable organs, the cost of recognizing the patient's rights may be too high for society to bear."

If a patient with unusual bodily substances is encouraged (as he or she will be, by today's decision) to shop around for the highest bid on the patient's spleen, tissue, blood, or other bodily substance, the quality of health care and medical research undoubtedly will suffer. By recognizing a property right in such substances, and expanding informed consent to include advisement of potential research and commercial use of the matter removed from the patient's body, the majority clearly establishes a right to bargain over body parts and share in the financial windfall that sometimes ensues from years of expensive medical research.

The right to be advised of research and commercial use of substances taken from one's body implies the right to withhold consent for such use. As one of many illustrations of the potential ramifications of the majority's ruling, we need consider only the current massive effort to eradicate the lethal AIDS virus. Any determination granting a patient the unilateral right to forbid the use of tissues and fluids, already taken from his or her body, in research designed to find a cure to a disease posing a grave threat to public health, should be left to the Legislature. It should also be noted that the problems of consent, and of "profit-sharing," are compounded where specimens from several individuals (or perhaps several hundred or several thousand) are utilized in effecting a cure for a deadly disease.

Much of the New Jersey Supreme Court's characterization of "baby-bartering" in the celebrated case of *Matter of Baby M.* (1988) 109 N.J. 396, 537 A.2d 1227 is equally applicable to "body-part bargaining": "The evils inherent in baby-bartering are loathsome for a myriad of reasons. The child is sold.... Baby-selling potentially results in the exploitation of all parties involved." "Whatever idealism may have motivated any of the participants, the profit motive predominates, permeates, and ultimately governs the transaction. The demand for children is great and the supply small.... The situation is ripe for the entry of the middleman who will bring some equilibrium into the market by increasing the supply through the use of money." "There are, in a civilized society, some things that money cannot buy.... There are, in short, values that society deems more important than granting to wealth whatever it can buy, be it labor, love, or life."

* * *

Notes and Questions

1. In 1990, the Supreme Court of California reversed the Court of Appeals, holding that Mr. Moore did not have a cause of action for conversion but that he had properly stated a cause of action for breach of fiduciary duty and lack of informed consent, thereby keeping alive the property rights questions raised in this Chapter. The line of *Moore* cases clearly presents the issues of who should have the right to a living patient's body parts once removed and, if that right is to be given to the patient, whether that right should be protected by a property rule, a liability rule, or a rule of inalienability.

Question: Taking into account the various considerations raised in this section, what rule is most consistent with the goal of efficiency?

2.   Mr. Moore was alive and competent before and after his spleen was removed.   Many body parts used for transplantation are removed from individuals who are legally dead.   42 U.S.C. § 274e(a) (1989) provides that:

It shall be unlawful for any person to knowingly acquire, receive, or otherwise transfer any human organ for valuable consideration for use in human transplantation if the transfer affects interstate commerce.

Section 274e(a) does not prohibit the use of organs for transplantation. It does, however, prohibit the *sale* of organs.

Questions: What is the effect of this statute on the supply of organs available for transplantation?   Is a rule of inalienability appropriate for organs removed from cadavers?   Does the analysis of such a case differ from the analysis of *Moore?*

Index

References are to Pages

---

†